Light: From Aten to Laser

Light

From Aten to Laser

Edited by Thomas B. Hess and John Ashbery

The Macmillan Company
New York

The light of day suffuses the sky, but
night has paradoxically invaded the earth
in René Magritte's *Domain of Lights,*
1953-54 (76¾ inches high; Guggenheim
Museum). First exploited by de Chirico,
the *angst* which an ambiguous source of light
causes in the spectator has been a favorite
theme of Metaphysical and Surrealist painting.

Cover: The apocalyptic vision of the *Resurrected Christ*, right-hand panel (98 inches high) of Matthias Grünewald's Isenheim Altarpiece, 1512-15 (Musée d'Unterlinden, Colmar) gives more the impression of an explosion than a simple effect of light. The huge yellow halo rimmed with blue and turning paler toward the center suggests a burst of gunpowder, which was then in use and its effects well-known.

Constable was the first great painter to take landscape painting out of the studio into the open air, and to substitute on-the-spot observation for notes and sketches. This is a detail from his *Salisbury Cathedral from the Bishop's Garden*, 1826, © Frick Collection, New York.

Art News is published
ten times a year, September-June;
and Art News Annual (incorporating Portfolio)
each October, by Newsweek, Inc.
Address: 444 Madison Avenue, New York, N.Y. 10022
Telephone: TE 8-3730. Cables: Artenews, New York

Art News is published
ten times a year, September-June;
and Art News Annual (incorporating Portfolio)
each October, by Newsweek, Inc.
Address: 444 Madison Avenue, New York, N.Y. 10022
Telephone: TE 8-3730. Cables: Artenews, New York

Art News Annual is distributed for
Newsweek, Inc. by The Macmillan Company,
866 Third Avenue, New York, N.Y. 10022.

Contents

10   *The Eye of Ra*
By Kim Levin

20   *Generation of Light 1945-1969*
By Scott Burton

34   *Gothic Glass*
By Florens Deuchler

44   *Byzantium: Gold and Light*
By John Beckwith

58   *The Outer Light*
By Gabriel Laderman

72   *In the Light of Dreams*
By Nicolas Calas and Elena Calas

84   *The Last Cathedral*
By Robert Descharnes and Clovis Prévost

96   *The Discovery of Night*
By Michael Mahoney

108   *What Color is Divine Light?*
By Patrik Reuterswärd

128   *Literal Light*
By John Perreault

142   *Electric Poetry*
By Aram Saroyan

Sunset between the pyramids of Cheops and Khefre at Giza, Egypt. On the shortest day of the year when the sun seemed to be dying, the pyramids were at their brightest, gleaming like mirrors as though to revivify Ra, the Sun God. Photograph by Kim Levin.

146   Index
147   Credits
148   Advertisements

Limestone fragment of a sunk relief with royal bust on a standard, symbol of kingship; 2nd century B.C., 10 inches high, Brooklyn Museum.

When lit from the rear (left), shadows on the sunk relief obliterate the delicate profile, but proper lateral light brings out the details, suggesting that such sculpture was meant to be seen at a specific time of day.

By Kim Levin

The Eye of Ra

At Sakkara, a few miles southwest of modern Cairo, a statue of the 3rd Dynasty king Zoser was found sitting enclosed in a small box-like room next to his pyramid. For 46 centuries the king—the golden Horus, son of Ra—had gazed out through two peepholes, his rock-crystal eyeballs glowing in the sunlight.

The sun, like the eye, makes things visible, and the sun to ancient Egyptians was the eye of the god Ra. It was also a golden falcon, a dung-beetle rolling an incandescent globe or simply a flattened disk. It was Ra Horakhte on the horizon, Khepre rising, Ra at noon, Atum setting, or the abstract Aten in a sky made of metal. It traveled across the sky in a boat, it flew as a bird, it was swallowed every evening by, and born every morning from, a sky goddess who was sometimes a woman and sometimes a cow. After dark it progressed on an elaborate and perilous journey through the separate hours of the night. Its daily birth was assisted by baboons (the roosters of Egypt) shrieking just before dawn, as it rose between two luminous mountains or on a horizon guarded by two lions. At the beginning of time it was hatched from an egg, cradled in a lotus flower. Its rays were rows of overlapping triangles or lotus flowers, or—during the Amarna period—numerous lines ending in human hands. The flesh of the gods was made of gold—their bones were silver—and gold, incorruptible, was equated with the sun's rays, both giving divine life and revivifying by their touch. All myths, all images, all gods, eventually connected to the sun.

The sun was and is the unavoidable fact of life in Egypt: pervasive, unrelenting and daily. When light is a matter of flicking a switch it is easy to forget that its prime source is the sun. The quantity of sunlight in Egypt is extraordinary; so is the quality: it is blinding, high-contrast light, light that can be felt as scorching heat in the nostrils—step into a

shadow and it is instantly cool. Dawn and sunset are sudden, brief, spectacular.

Yet light is a subject that has usually been ignored by modern Egyptologists. Only one site, Abu Simbel, has been studied in terms of light; and there is only one book[1] that considers the role of light in Egyptian temples. Egyptian art is so massive—so dense with materiality and sheer size—that what we tend to see is only its solidity, its formalism, its "minimalness." But the destructions of time make what we see partial, incomplete. What the Egyptians saw was the animating presence of light. And not only did they make images of the sun in its various forms, they incorporated its actual light in their art.

Everywhere among the remnants of ancient Egypt are hints of this fundamental awareness of light—materials that attract and reflect the sun, luminous surfaces that gleam, glitter, glow, shine. Obelisks were capped in gold and some were completely sheathed with it. Pyramids were faced with shiny white limestone that gleamed dazzlingly bright in the sunlight; one, for at least half its height, was of a shiny rose-pink granite described by early Arab writers as "like satin." Temple floors were sometimes surfaced with electrum, and certain columns and doorjambs were garnished with gold. Statues were of highly polished hard black basalt or translucent alabaster; those of gods were gold-covered. There are Old Kingdom statues with inlaid eyeballs of quartzite and rock crystal and New Kingdom lamps of translucent calcite. There is Akhenaten's sun worship and Tutankhamon's gold—and even some small gold sequins covered with a transparent film that reflects as purple when light hits them. And at Abu Simbel, Rameses' temple is oriented so that the rising sun penetrates its interior on special days.

Temples

The most elaborate of the daily temple rituals took place at dawn, at the time of the sun's birth, and were ceremonies of washing and purification, involving the sacred lake (the rectangular sheet of water being a natural reflector), before exposing the statue of the god to the sun's light to revivify it. Briefer rituals were celebrated at midday and sunset, but

Kim Levin did graduate work in Egyptian art and archeology at Columbia and recently spent two summers making a film in Egypt. She is a painter with two one-man shows in New York to her credit (both at the Poindexter Gallery) and is a regular critic for ARTnews.

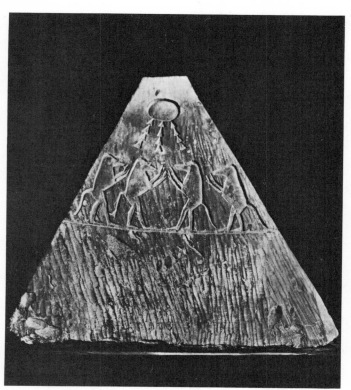

Baboons were the roosters of Egypt, their cries assisted the dawn; in this Late Period pyramidion in the Louvre, they are seen worshipping the sun and receiving its rays.

Osiris depicted on a bier at the foot of a light shaft; when the sun's rays penetrate the opening, they bathe the god's body, manifesting his rebirth; Temple of Denderah.

Diorite statue of Khefre, 4th Dynasty, discovered by Mariette in the king's valley temple; a falcon, symbol of the sun, cradles the king's head (Cairo Museum).

Monumental statue of the 3rd Dynasty King Zoser; it faced two peepholes through which light streamed and illuminated its rock-crystal eyeballs (Cairo Museum).

The emphasis on lighting in Egyptian temples is seen at Edfu, where the original Ptolemaic ceiling remains; it was pierced to let light fall upon the sanctuary walls.

it was the rising sun on the horizon that was most important, the moment of the light's appearance out of darkness: the triumph of the luminous east versus the maleficent west.

Akhenaten named his city Akhetaten, "*akhet*" meaning "realm of light" or "horizon." His temples had no roofs; they were open to the sun. Akhenaten let light flood in direct, uncontrolled, but this was the exception. His heresy was in making the Aten (a minor sun-god of Heliopolis) the exclusive god, and in taking the mystery out of light. Before and after his time, temples were traditionally dim, roofed with stone, windowless. The further one penetrated, the dimmer they became. Not only dimmer, but the ceiling of each successive chamber was lower and the floor higher, the corridors narrower and the chambers smaller with less space and more columns, narrowing to almost total darkness in the sanctuary with its statue of the god, creating a

sense of enclosure and darkened mystery in a bright land edged by limitless deserts.

Because scholars are so silent about the subject of light, one might almost conclude that darkness was most important to the ancient Egyptians. But it wasn't. The traditional interest was in controlled light: in limited, directed, visible beams of light; in reflected light; in sudden rhythmic contrasts between light and dark. At the huge temple of Karnak, dim halls alternated with bright sunlit courtyards, the alternation quickening as the areas got progressively smaller, creating a kind of mammoth strobe effect; anyone entering passed ever more rapidly from light to darkness to light to darkness.

In the dark temples, light entered through small slits in the roof. These rectangular or square apertures—narrow at the top and wide at the bottom like truncated pyramids—

13

channeled the sunlight through a pinpoint source and directed it in a spotlight shaft onto a specific object: statue or sanctuary. As early as the 4th Dynasty, the rows of polished black statues of King Khefre in his valley temple at Giza—the famous Khefre with a falcon behind his head was one of these—were illuminated by such spotlighting from oblique slits cut at the juncture of wall and roof. The floor of this temple was of alabaster, reflecting and diffusing the light. At Edfu and Denderah, some 2,400 years later, light from similar slits still illuminated the sanctuary. At Edfu, reliefs in the window embrasures of the stairways represent the sun's rays as rows of truncated triangles, carved at angles parallel to the entering light. At Denderah, the sun's rays fall on reliefs of the dead Osiris, reviving him symbolically.

The orientation of the temple of Rameses II at Abu Simbel, where the doorway is the only source of light, was thoroughly studied before it was moved. The rising sun first illuminates a row of baboons at the top of the façade, then moves down, lighting up the hawk-faced sun-god over the door and the colossal statues of Rameses, and finally the doorway itself, gradually penetrating the portal into the temple at certain times of year. On two days—October 19 and February 21—it reaches the inner sanctuary (200 feet in)

where there are four seated statues. The two sun gods, Ra and Amon, and Rameses between them, are then lit by the sun. The fourth statue, of Ptah, god of the underworld, remains in darkness. Near the temple was a small roofless chapel with baboons and obelisks dedicated to Ra Horakhte, sun-god of the horizon, and it was oriented so that the sun rose exactly between its two pylons on the winter solstice, the day of the god's annual rebirth.[2]

Other temples also must have been related to the sun. Their pylons, symbolizing the two luminous mountains between which the sun supposedly rose, were described as "shining like the horizon of heaven." In the course of the day, the sun illuminated one part after another of their exteriors—exteriors covered with relief sculpture, for which the source of lighting is vital. Relief can be blotted out by direct light or disfigured by light from the wrong direction. The inscriptions, cut very deep, are visible all day, while the reliefs undergo gradual transformations, some being visible only at certain times or only in summer when the sun is high. It is possible that the subject-matter and the time of its visibility were correlated.

Because most roofs no longer exist, we don't know when or if the light entered through the doorways, but there is

Entrance to the Temple of Luxor where an obelisk surmounts attendant baboons; note the fast alternations of light and shade in the colonnade, creating a giant strobe effect.

Penetrating an Egyptian temple, corridors narrow and light gets dimmer until you reach the darkness of the sanctuary: inner court of the Rameside Medinet Habu Temple.

Only twice a year, on October 19 and February 21, sunlight floods the inner sanctuary of the Temple of Rameses II at Abu Simbel. In this record of such an event by photographer Georg Gerster, the sun-god Ra (with headdress) and Rameses are fully visible.

strong evidence, previously overlooked, that it did. In Egyptian temples, sunk relief (carved beneath the surface-plane of the stone) is used for exterior surfaces because it shows up better than raised relief in strong sunlight. Raised relief is used for interior surfaces. But on the front faces of interior doorjambs between chambers, we find that sunk relief was used. It is probable therefore that the direct light of the sun must have sometimes entered and fallen on these doorjambs as it penetrated to the sanctuary. At Karnak, and maybe elsewhere, these front faces of doorjambs leading to the sanctuary were covered in gold-leaf, possibly to reinforce the effect of the sunlight, or to substitute for it.

Perhaps the most unexpected optical effect produced by the Egyptians can still be seen at Karnak in a small dark chamber in the temple of Ptah. The chamber is lit only by a small opening (in the usual truncated pyramid shape) in the center of the ceiling, admitting a cone of peculiarly bluish light that envelops and illumines the statue beneath it. The archeologist Legrain observed in 1916 that it also creates an incredible optical illusion: the room is a "camera obscura" similar to that described in the Renaissance by Giovanni Battista della Porta. The blue light is a projection of the sky, and on cloudy days the moving image of the passing clouds is projected onto the statue, appearing to advance as if the god residing in the statue had become

manifest. "The faithful could no longer doubt that their prayers were heard or rejected when they saw 'the divinity' become animate, turn white, blue, and out of the white light advance silently toward them, then suddenly disappear," said Legrain, who mentions that there were other similar chambers.[3]

Obelisks

From Pliny to the 19th century, the obelisk was said to represent a ray of the sun, a fact which is rarely mentioned today, though not denied. Obelisks always occur at places of sun-worship: at Heliopolis, at the sun temple of Abu Gurab, much later at Karnak and Luxor. Early ones are squat; later they are more tapered. They are usually on the east bank of the Nile, and their inscriptions always refer to the rising sun, which is not surprising because, made of rose granite and tipped in gold, they heralded the dawn, reflecting the light of the rising sun from their pyramid-shaped tips before its rays lit the ground, as if predicting its arrival.

Obelisks were said to derive their shape from the oldest and most sacred object in Egypt, the *benben* stone at Heliopolis. According to legends, the sun god or the phoenix alighted at dawn on the *benben*. The phoenix is

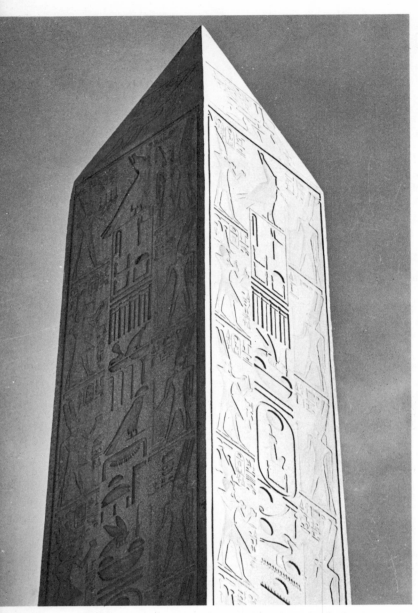

Obelisks often were tipped with gold and caught the first rays of the sunrise while the ground was still in shadows; this one, dedicated to Hatshepsut, is at Karnak.

represented by the Egyptians as a large pale-blue bird, and there exists at least one representation of it emitting a halo or blue light. Little is known about the *benben,* but the legend might contain more fact than fiction.

Since the obelisk is a prismatic shape—four-sided and tapering, shifting its angle at the top to converge to a point—and since the Egyptians obtained other sophisticated effects by simple means, it is not impossible that the *benben* could have been made out of a highly polished semi-transparent stone such as calcite or quartz,[4] and have functioned as an imperfect prism, separating white light into colors. The blue end of the spectrum, bending most, would be most likely to separate visibly through such a prism. At dawn, the sun's rays would strike an obelisk-shaped prism at an angle such that a momentary flash of

The Eye of Ra

blue light would be emitted. Perhaps this is the meaning of the blue phoenix and its blue halo.

Pyramids

The obelisk was sometimes depicted in hieroglyphs with the sun on its point as if perched upon it: it was thought of as the throne for the rising sun, as well as its ray. So the pyramid might have been the tomb for the setting sun. From the site of Memphis, the ancient capital, it is sometimes possible to see the sun set behind the Great Pyramid as if impaled on its point or swallowed into it; other times it sets between the Great Pyramid and the pyramid of Khefre. On what days and from which ancient sites does the sun set into the points of the various pyramids? It may be significant—no one has considered it.

Pyramids supposedly derive their shape from the tip of the obelisk, and were said to represent the sun's rays slanting toward the four cardinal points of the earth. Travelers have noticed the resemblance: "A remarkable spectacle may sometimes be seen in the late afternoon of a cloudy winter day at Giza. When standing on the road to Sakkara and gazing westwards at the Pyramids' plateau, it is possible to see the sun's rays striking downwards through a gap in the clouds at about the same angle as the slope of the Great Pyramid," wrote I.E.S. Edwards[5] of the British Museum. The ancient Pyramid Texts confirm this visible image. "I have trodden those thy rays as a ramp under my feet whereon I mount up to that my mother, the living Ureus on the brow of Ra," reads Spell 508, and Spell 523 says, "Heaven hath strengthened for thee the rays of the sun in order that thou mayest lift thyself to heaven as the eye of Ra." In ancient Egypt each pyramid had a name, and several refer to light—"Snefru Gleams," "The Luminous Mountain Horizon of Cheops," "Merenra Is Luminous and Beautiful." Today even without their smooth white facing they catch the sun; originally they must have been very bright reflectors. And since the sun's rays were often represented as strings of triangles, and since light openings in temples were hollowed-out pyramidal shapes, the pyramids' association with light would seem secure.

Yet archeologists are suspicious of searches for meaning. Considering the wild fantasies of the Victorians about Egypt and particularly about the pyramids, this formalist reaction is understandable. People who have theories about the pyramids are known, among Egyptologists, as Pyramidiots.

The accepted view today is that pyramids are nothing more than the tombs of kings—in spite of the fact that often empty sealed sarcophagi rather than real burials have been found in them. It is also acknowledged that since pyramids were connected to temples, they had something to do with worship, probably of the dead king. The pyramids have been studied purely in terms of geometry, showing that their sides are oriented with incredible precision toward north, south, east and west, and that their slopes remain remarkably exact, and that each of the three pyramids at Giza embodies a mathematical concept usually credited to later times—the Golden Section, the Pythagorean triangle and the 8:5 Isosceles. Flinders Petrie mentioned that certain long narrow trenches on the east slope of Khefre's pyramid were a device for observing transits of stars. It has also been proven by Badawy and Trimble that two non-functional "air shafts" angling up from the burial chamber of Cheops' pyramid to its north and south slopes were aimed respectively toward the north polar stars (known as the Imperishable Ones and venerated because they never vanished beneath the horizon) and toward Orion. Badawy concludes that they were designed as trajectories for aiming the soul of the dead king toward these stars. Prof. Alvarez is searching for hidden chambers with a cosmic ray detector, and even the geometry of the pyramids' shadows has been studied. Yet the pyramids themselves have not been considered as illuminated objects.

Except for the two at Dahshur, the Old Kingdom pyramids all incline at a slope of about 52°. The slope varies slightly from pyramid to pyramid, but remains constant for each one. Two, the Great Pyramid and the pyramid at Medum, have slopes of 51°50'. Archeologists don't know what determined the choice of this angle. It would seem to be a deliberate searching for an extreme exactness of angle, an exactness not necessitated by esthetic or technical considerations. Could it have been determined by a desire to catch the light in a certain way?

Following this thought, would the sun's rays ever hit a surface tilted at a slope of 52° at the latitude and longitude of Giza to give maximum reflection—that is, perpendicularly—and if so, when? The answer turns out that on one day only during the year will a slope of 52° catch the light directly: the day of the winter solstice, at noon, when the sun at Giza is at approximately 38°. The light would have reflected off the south slope which, at Giza, is the side visible from Memphis. So on the shortest darkest day of the year, when the sun was weakest, lowest in the sky, and

Pyramids at Giza: Khefre (below right) and Cheops; figures on the slopes of Cheops (above) indicate that it is as high as a 50-story building. Originally the sides were surfaced in gleaming white limestone which reflected the sunlight.

The Bent Pyramid of Snefru at Dahshur dates from the 4th Dynasty (2650-2500 B.C.); the change in slope, often considered a miscalculation, might have been deliberate.

17

might seem to be dying, the pyramids were at their brightest, gleaming like mirrors held up to the sky, as if sending light back to the sun to revivify it, just as the rays of the sun supposedly revivified the statue of the god, giving it life when they touched it, and the gold of Tutankhamon supposedly guaranteed him eternal life.

At Dahshur one pyramid slopes at an angle of about 43°; the other, the "Bent Pyramid," starts with a slope slightly greater than 52°, and shifts to a slope of 43°. This shift in angle is sometimes said to be due to miscalculation or haste, but this too could be deliberate. The 43° slope would reflect maximum light on two days—one in October, the other in February—when the sun is perpendicular to it, at 47°. These two days might prove, with the aid of a computer, to coincide with the days the light penetrated Abu Simbel, October 19 and February 21. If this proved to be so, there could be no possible doubt that 4,600 years ago—some 1,200 years before Akhenaten's sun worship, 1,400 years before Abu Simbel was built—actual light was an integral part of the concept of the pyramids, specific and exact.

Today Egyptian guides ingeniously light the interiors of tombs for tourists by angling mirrors to reflect the sun, *Son et Lumière* plays on the pyramids at night, government buildings are outlined in green neon on holidays and King Zoser sits in the Cairo Museum. The ancient Egyptians also used light in temples, on obelisks and pyramids to create spectacular illusions and theatrical effects, but they showed a fine disregard for the spectator. Their light effects—and their paintings and objects hidden in tombs—were not meant for the public but for participants. Their use of light was sequential, serial, cyclical—a shaft of light or a reflection, an apparition that appears, moves across a surface or onto an object, at certain times, on certain days, at a particular site, or only if there is a cloud overhead. Imagine the effect a deliberate controlled beam could have had when the sun was not only the source of light, but a watchful god, and its rays, his direct emanation.

1. J. L. de Cenival, *Living Architecture: Egyptian,* New York, 1964.
2. J.K. van der Haagen, "Rameses' Mysterious Encounter at Dawn," *UNESCO Courier,* Oct. 1962.
3. G. Legrain, "Observation d'un Phénomène Optique," *Annales du Service des antiquités de l'Egypte,* v.16, 1916.
4. Both were readily available. A few tiny glass obelisks from Egypt exist (their purpose is unknown), but the early Egyptians didn't, as far as we know, have transparent glass. Rock quartz or calcite would have served as well—modern prisms are often made of them.
5. I.E.S. Edwards, *The Pyramids of Egypt,* Baltimore, 1947.

Funerary papyrus scroll of the 21st Dynasty princess Her-uben, ca. 1050 B.C.; in this detail the princess (right) and a sacred baboon worship the rising sun (Cairo Museum).

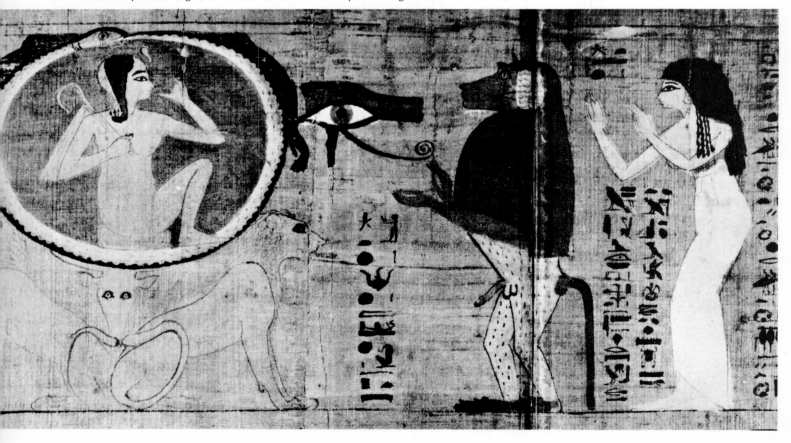

Back of the throne of King Tutankhamun, wood covered with gold leaf and glass and stone inlays; the scene is set in the hall of the palace; the sun (Aten) sends down its rays, ending in hands, on the king, while the queen anoints him with perfume.

A metaphysical concern for light as time is underscored by the clock and the title of Edward Hopper's *Seven A. M.*, 1948, 30 inches high. Whitney Museum, New York.

High noon of black-and-white: Franz Kline's *New York*, 1953, 79 inches high. Albright-Knox Gallery, Buffalo, N.Y.

A masterpiece of the postwar wave of black-and-white painting in America: Willem de Kooning's *Night Square*, 1949, enamel, 30 inches high. Jackson Gallery, New York.

By Scott Burton

Generation of Light 1945-1969

As does the painting of any period, post-World War II American art necessarily concerns itself with the depiction of luminosity; but really not to the degree that it can be said to be a unifying concern, and to a much lesser degree than many other movements and styles. The eternal element of light has, however, been as thoroughly reinvestigated and put to individual use by American painters as have been the elements inseparable from it of color, in particular; form, shape and scale; and method and concept. The profusion of innovations in the quarter-century of our art from the mid-1940s through the late '60s may have resulted in no theoretical homogeneity, especially in regard to light as a pictorial concept; but, and paradoxically, few phases of modernism have been marked by such sustained intensity in the exploration of luminosity. The achievements of our painters are diverse, but they are continuously brilliant.

For hundreds of years, "light" in Western art meant, of course, essentially one thing—the convention of tonality, the system of value gradations whose function is to represent volumes and the spaces around them. When Turner and then the Impressionists freed light from its schematic identity as the opposite of "dark," they opened the way to our century's purely chromatic painting, for which luminosity is a result of the temperature and degree of saturation of hues, and therefore not quantifiable or subject to formulization but exclusively a matter of personal sensibility. Sensibilities have genealogies, and some case can be made, in the period here under discussion, for two major kinds of American light: one is urban, hard, often hyper-brilliant, artificial-looking; the other is pastoral, natural, much more atmospheric and "slow" or dim. Both are referential, both cut across stylistic and historical boundaries, both are generated by temperamental affinities of which the artists may even be unaware.

But before tracing these two main currents, we must remember that chromatic abstraction, whatever its "feel," is quite recent. Preceding it are both the late paintings of Edward Hopper, the last survivor of the first chapter of American modernism; and the well-documented, early phase of

Scott Burton teaches at the School of Visual Arts, New York, and his articles appear regularly in ARTnews.

the second chapter—that is, the "black-and-white" period of Abstract-Expressionism whose zenith was around 1950 and whose first and last, as well as greatest, masters were Willem de Kooning and Franz Kline. By different means, both Hopper and the black and white abstractionists provide a clear demarcation for later developments beyond tonality. The dialectical language of light-dark as used in a Hopper such as *Seven A.M.*, 1948, presents no critical problems, but it is a typically important and relevant painting for its metaphysical concern with light as time. The value system in it is entirely "retrograde," innocent of coloristic self-sufficiency, but Hopper is as precise and serious about his "anecdotal" light as Monet ever was about his purely observed light. The observer-less, closed off view is not only made more intense by the numerous darkening and brightening surfaces and recesses, but, with the quasi-eponymous clock, is raised to a transcendent illustrationalism as ambiguous and enigmatic as any Surrealist scene. Hopper's modernity is obvious in his smooth unification of Cubistic geometry and representationalism, but perhaps less apparent—and even more interesting today—is his emblematic or metaphoric bent, accounting for the unique notion of light, translated into time (a specific time of day), as the true subject of the painting. The straightforward American realist has Pirandellian depths.

Curiously, the painting least like Hopper's of the same period—the wholly post-European art of the New York School, first generation—is fundamentally similar in its conception of light as value. De Kooning's *Night Square*, painted one year later than the Hopper, is also a tonal painting, yet it is a paradigm of the most advanced work of the time. Though its value scale is reduced to the simplest and most total contrast possible, pure black and pure white, *Night Square* exhibits an amazing multiplicity of luministic virtuosity within its bare, polarized means. De Kooning creates a light of sharp, dramatically shifting "shadows," obscure hollows and sudden, dazzling streaks of radiance which seem to come from behind the darkness as often as they split or float in it. The unpredictable interstices and dissociated lines of white act peculiarly in that they do not illuminate or lessen the darkness but rather seem to increase it; de Kooning's recurring tendency toward somber coloration (as in his *Men* and some of the earlier *Women*) is, though coexistent with an equally strong impulse toward coloristic exuberance, never more affecting than in his strange, murkily pristine black and whites. Along with Hopper and the whole Western tradition of light as value, de Kooning organizes here in a light-to-dark scheme, yet this is not *grisaille* painting but an art which conceives of black and white as two colors, or uses them so.

To jump ahead in de Kooning's career, we see the proof of this in such masterpieces of the 1960s as *Rosy-Fingered Dawn at Louse Point* (see colorplate). The allusions in the title to both Homeric pre-history and the local geography of the artist's Long Island habitat point up the matutinal

freshness of his art after the dark-edged, charcoal-etched *Women* of the '50s. The purity and openness of *Rosy-Fingered Dawn,* with its pink, yellow and white skin, are prefigured in such de Koonings as the 1939 *Elegy* or the 1945 *Pink Angels,* but new for the artist—and for American art—after the late '50s is the spiritual hedonism of organizing the painting wholly in terms of light. What unifies it, including its minor passages of greens, is the same thing which holds the black and white pictures together: sheer luminosity. Drawing, gesture, planar space—all are subsumed into an overriding brilliance, here as clear and untroubled as *Night*

From de Kooning's freest, most pastoral phase: *Rosy-Fingered Dawn at Louse Point,* 1963, 80 inches high. Stedelijk Museum, Amsterdam.

Mark Rothko: *No. 8, 1952,* 80½ inches high. Rothko's light is the most atmospheric among the first-generation color-field painters. Collection of Mr. and Mrs. Burton Tremaine, Meriden, Conn.

Sharp and soft verticals contrast in the non-atmospheric but light-filled field of Barnett Newman's *Vir Heroicus Sublimis,* 1950-51, 95⅜ inches high. Museum of Modern Art, New York.

In his untitled 1957 painting (79 inches high), Ad Reinhardt equalizes tone to the point of obscuring forms.

Square is tense and puzzling. In both moods, de Kooning's synthesizing principle is that of light; for all his spatial ambiguities and internal contradictions, he makes in both cases an optical world held together by form-obliterating radiance.

After de Kooning, the master of "no-color" was Kline, whose equally tonal light is bleaker and harsher than that of the several other painters who eliminated color from their palettes around the same time. Kline, with his great awkward

structures which are at the same time black armatures in white voids, white forms in a far-reaching darkness and planes of paint overlapping in a shallow space or in no space at all, is a Ryder of noon instead of midnight, and the heir of Eakins and Homer, native geniuses of unremitting, almost tragic clarity in their charged, oppressive pictures. Kline's broad, iris-confounding swaths of extreme brilliance and fathomless dark are not only the high noon of American black and white art, but also its twilight, for after Kline, no gestural abstraction is able to produce light as well as form from this binary resource.

The resource of color was of course never absent, even in the purgative period of black and white painting. Indeed, the American who comes at once to mind when the subject of light in American art is raised is Mark Rothko, who not only never eliminated color but elevated it to an unprecedented importance. Rothko's incandescent blocks of color-light, whether in the typically warm orange, yellow and white of *No. 8, 1952* (see colorplate) or in the cooler, shadowy blue and submarine green paintings (which together led to the experiments with a palette of heated obscurity of the later '50s and the '60s), are notable for their avoidance of exaggerated value contrasts as well as for their nearly explicit imagery of land- and seascape. The armatures—the soft frame around the perimeters of the individual color squares or around the entire work—and the sparely used horizontal stripes (like the blue in *No. 8, 1952*) are more differentiated on the scale of hues, departing just enough in value from

White canvas shines through as light in Hans Hofmann's *Memoria in Aeternum*, 1962, 84 inches high. Museum of Modern Art.

Philip Guston's *Painting*, 1954, 60⅛ inches high, is one of the high points of "Abstract-Impressionism." Museum of Modern Art.

their neighboring tones to perform a structural, "holding" function without, however, threatening by over-articulation the tentative existences of the colors weightlessly and as if momentarily settled upon the fragile surfaces. The steady, even light in a Rothko is its most tranquil element, whether in a super-radiant key or invisibly dark; the rest is reticent to an anxious-making degree. Rothko's tonalities are limited in their variety, necessarily reduced so that no wrenching will take place, no discreteness, but instead a recessive and underplayed adjustment of value, tending toward equalization and serving the needs of the colors themselves (without giving up atmosphere in favor of "pure" or flat color). In Rothko, light is made one with color and atmosphere; for this commanding synthesis, he is a pivotal figure between the Impressionist inheritance and the American painting of the 1960s, a seminal artist whose progeny include such diverse younger painters as Ralph Humphrey, Agnes Martin, Ray Parker and other "romantic Minimalists," who uncannily combine defined edge or contour with abstract *sfumato*.

Among other major painters of the generation of de Kooning and Rothko, the non-gestural or "field-painting" wing of the New York School is further divided over the question of atmosphere. Rothko is the master of airiness; of his conceptual colleagues, Newman has shown less interest in atmosphere, Reinhardt was not to pursue it intensively until the latter part of his career, and Still's impulses took him in an anti-atmospheric direction.

Barnett Newman's work is hardly without light, however.

The jarring verticals of color that split his monolithic façades represent, especially at their brightest as in *Vir Heroicus Sublimis,* an entirely new use of light in painting. Later to be explored by Larry Poons, most thoroughly, and also by many Pop and Op artists, Newman's color-light is presented in an epiphanic structure. The verticals exist as light only for an instant; the "illumination" is short-lived and soon the eye reduces the immaterial flash to corporeal pigment. However, scanning the vast surfaces, we then pick up once again in our peripheral vision the elusive, intermittent glow of the narrow stripes. Newman's light possesses an insight-like structure; it is momentary and recurrent, though not at the viewer's own will. While Newman's feeling for the value range is less strong than his unique sense of the optical volume of color, he is able, in his best works, to maintain a sourceless radiance throughout even the largest areas. This light coexists with the occasional blinding perpendiculars, rather than emerging from them. The middle-value stripes are generally related to the field tonally, and to the brighter stripes formally, and so they act as intermediaries between light—the immaterial—and the material color-covered surface; this accounts perhaps for their ghostliness and even for Newman's invention of his strange "non-stripe," a form made by painting brushily across masking tape, then pulling off the tape so that there are two scumbled columns around an empty center. These negative stripes are as light-conducting as are the positive verticals.

Clyfford Still seems a peculiarly lusterless artist, as it were; the disturbing body of his thick patches of paint, which exist

Morris Louis: *Floral*, 1959, 101 inches high. The luminosity of white canvas is never fully hidden by Louis' thin films of color. Collection of Mrs. Marcella Louis, Washington, D.C.

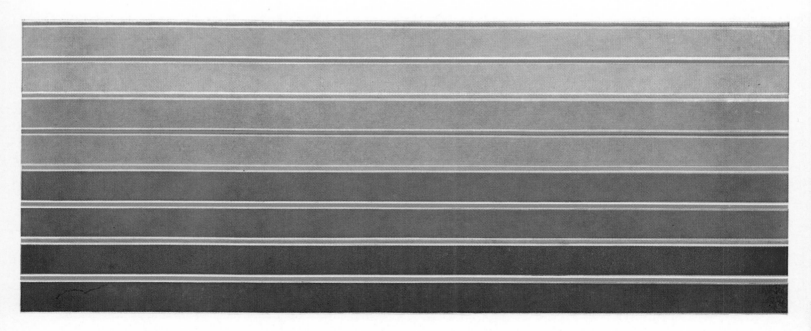

Kenneth Noland: *Stria*, 1967, 78 inches high. Noland's eye-filling, horizontally striped formats of recent years leave him free to concentrate on color relationships; the resultant light is fabulously clean. Caleb Steinberg collection, Denver.

as if in a state of peeling off or even sliding down the canvas-wall, have, I think, contributed importantly to the recent invention in three-dimensional American art of soft, shape-shifting, disarrayed objects, but (doubtless intentionally) Still has eliminated any impression of over-all luminosity, to say nothing of atmosphere, in his dry painting.

Ad Reinhardt also eliminates light, in the sense of brightness, but demonstrates that to do so is not to eliminate luminosity. From the time he reduced his forms to simple rectangles, he tended to make his colors, whether the reds of the early '50s or the later black-threshold browns, blues and greens, equal in value. Even before, in his over-all paintings, the light had been dim and constant throughout, but more and more intensely until his death, Reinhardt sought an even and low light in his poised, anticipatory symmetries whose luminosity is as vivid (and as atmospheric) as the most burning, Turner-esque Rothkos.

To compare the rectilinear art of Reinhardt to the brush-drawn style of Philip Guston is to see how light ignores formal boundaries; these extremely different artists are both painters for whom light is produced by atmospheric color relations. The "Abstract-Impressionism" of Guston's trembling blues and efflorescent cadmiums and roses of the earlier '50s has its source not only in French painting but also in the Mondrian of the waves and piers; Guston's constant swells of short verticals and horizontals, stroked and re-stroked with a restless hand, have an unfading shimmer which gathers in intensity (near the painting's center, usually) to provide another absolutely individual use of light as structure. It is impossible to tell whether

the characteristic blues and reds mix more optically or more tactilely, but in any case we do not see such sheer luminosity successfully performing a structural function again until Jules Olitski's spray paintings and Sally Hazelet Drummond's mottled centrifugalities of flecks of color-light. Guston has, since this "sunrise" period, turned to more separable figure-ground relations and more contrasted light-dark relations, and his light is now generally much deeper and foggier; but in his thoroughgoing identification of color, light, form and surface, he is a virtuoso of atmospheric light. He is insufficiently recognized for his early synthesis of gestural and colorist modes of abstract painting.

Perhaps the most ambitious American painter in this respect, the one most eager to synthesize modes, was Hans Hofmann, whose visual bombast in his most Teutonically rhapsodic manner has unfortunately obliterated for some his authentically sensitive, more thinly and freely handled paintings of the late years. Hofmann was crucial in American art not only for the living example he provided of post-Fauve coloration, of the "push and pull" of pure color, creating a non-tonal luminosity, but also for his pioneering incorporation of the whiteness of the canvas itself into the light of the picture. It has been made clear by various spokesmen for "stain painting" how the luminosity can come from behind the colors, but Hofmann, the champion of the "open" surface—one taken through the entire register, from heavy slabs of paint all the way to passages of untouched canvas—was as central (when he exercised a restraint in his attack) to this '60s style as were Jackson Pollock, James Brooks and, even earlier, Arshile Gorky in certain

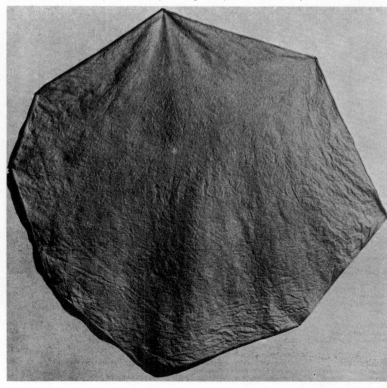

Richard Tuttle's *Canvas*, 1967, 54 inches high, dyed a single color, is the ultimate avatar of the technique of stain-painting. Betty Parsons Gallery, New York.

With its thin washes, Arshile Gorky's *The Plow and the Song*, 1947, 50¾ inches high is a luminous forerunner of stain-painting. **Allen** Museum, Oberlin, Ohio.

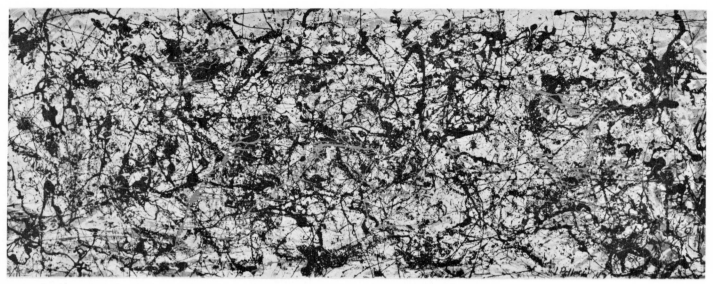

In *Lucifer*, 1947, 42 inches high, Jackson Pollock uses oil, enamel and aluminum paint to add reflected light on the surface to the gentler, diffuse light within. Collection Joseph H. Hazen, New York.

late paintings. When Hofmann washed an area so thinly that the canvas shone through with unhampered clarity, as he did as early as the mid-'40s in his Miroesque, automatist pictures, he pointed the way to a major new source of light in our art. The master of this kind of light was to be, of course, Morris Louis, whose lyrically clear voids of white brilliance contain the most translucent of colors in pools and tides which, even at their very deepest, rarely block all of the brilliant white ground.

A currently more emphasized precedent for Louis is Pollock,

for his innovative brush-eliminating procedure of paint application. Pollock's methodic revolution created, too, an important change in the quality of his own luminosity; he was the first to discover the strong but soft, dappled light characteristic of so much later American art. The undulatory rhythm of advancing and withdrawing spots of radiance, liquidly fused together, in such Pollocks as *Autumn Rhythm* or *Lavender Mist,* allows the artist to recreate, at will and without reference to actual landscape images, an effulgence as weightless as Rothko's, yet, remarkably, with a use of paint as forceful as

The light of literalism: Frank Stella's copper-covered *Ophir,* 1961, 90 inches high. James Holderbaum, Northampton, Mass.

Real shadows outline Gordon Hart's untitled acrylic on steel work, 1968, 67 inches high. Bykert Gallery, New York.

Rothko's is force-less. Pollock's indifference to calculated nuances of value is more than compensated by the omnipresence of his "visionary gleam," which is emitted from any and every point in the monumental suspended webs that mark his "classic" period.

Pollock's relentless search for the extreme boundaries of painting has provided American art of the 1960s with a further crucial precedent. So far, it has been light *in* painting that has been under discussion—i.e., depicted light—but with the advent of Minimal art, a practice of Pollock's which seems relatively minor to his total intention assumes a new relevance. I refer to his use of richly reflective paints. A number of artists had already painted with Ripolin or Duco enamels but Pollock, (after abandoning his brief habit of forgetting cigarette stubs and paint tube tops in his surfaces) was the first American to use aluminum paint for its literalistic, surface-emphasizing property. The metallic threads in many Pollocks—from *Cathedral* and *Lucifer,* 1947, to *White Light,* 1954—reflect rather than represent light; Pollock's unprecedented deployment of light *on* the painting (instead of *in* it) takes us directly to the Frank Stellas of the aluminum, copper and metallic monochrome series.

Along with his increasing assault on the rectangular format of orthodox thickness, the earlier Stella underscores the flatness or "realness" of his paintings to such a degree that they embrace one of the conditions of sculpture, its control of light with surface, almost leaving painting behind. Stella's near-sculptures are a link between Pollock's emphasis on presence (and the antecedent collage tradition) and the later work of young artists like David Novros, on whose iridescent Fiberglass wall units the light of literalism shines brightly, or like Gordon Hart, who approaches even closer the brink of "objecthood." Hart's flat, white rectangles (of steel plating), which are flush to the wall like paintings but supported by the floor like sculpture, depend on light, on *actual* light, for their very definition:

Ellsworth Kelly's *Blue Green Red I,* 1965, 108 inches high, is both "literal" and traditionally oriented. Stedelijk Museum, Amsterdam.

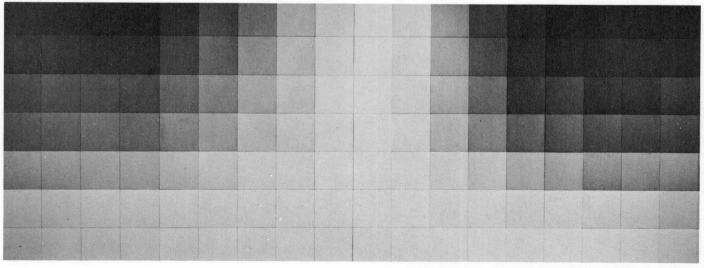

Robert Swain's *Untitled No. 2,* 1968, 91 inches high, deals explicitly and systematically with chromatic light. Fischbach Gallery, New York.

A *reductio ad absurdum* of tonality: Roy Lichtenstein's
Modern Painting Diptych, 1967, 48 inches high. Artist's collection.

without our discernment of the penumbral shadows of the
three edges not touching the floor, we are likely to miss entirely these pure white planes.

But the painting of the late '40s and the '50s does not lead
only in this direction—that is, toward literalism. Kenneth No-

land and Ellsworth Kelly, though they both have relied heavily
on physicality, still address themselves to "traditional" problems of painting. They seem increasingly (in today's context
of "advanced" art's wholesale embrace of three-dimension-
ality) both more conservative and more successful. Noland,

Larry Poons's *Richmond Ruckus,* 1963-64, 60 inches high, induces
optical after-images of high intensity. Brooks Baron, New York.

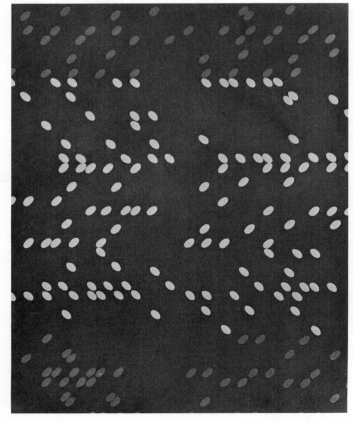

Sally Hazelet Drummond: *Beige Painting,* 1967, 28 inches high,
employs light compositionally. James T. Hill, New York.

particularly, improves as he eliminates eccentric formats and large areas of unpainted canvas in favor of post-systematic, intuitively colored canvases. His enormous, eye-filling but not unconventionally proportioned support shapes, horizontally striped in the last few years (as in *Stria,* see colorplate), leave him free to concentrate on relationships of color to color; the resultant light is fabulously clean and somewhat more atmospheric than his Pop-tinged earlier palette. The exclusive horizontality of recent Noland suggests landscape, and perhaps not coincidentally, one feels a new cogency in Noland's art, replacing earlier, uneasy mixture of hard, fast urban sensibility and the more romantic staining, derived from Louis. Stain painting was a procedure invented, after all, under the pressures of Louis' more hermetic and contemplative, not to say lyric, temperament; and Noland's is not Louis' character. His art will never possess the resonance of Louis', but his most recent period is his happiest—a new harmony of light, color and surface offers itself in an amplitude of fertile variations. The thin translucent color in recent Noland has a painterly vibrancy no longer interrupted by conflicting demands of overly emphatic actuality or temperamental ambivalence.

More direct heirs of the Pollock-Hofmann-Louis staining are young innovators like Richard Tuttle, who goes beyond it to actual dyeing—a thorough, total saturation of the fabric. In Tuttle's wrinkled octagons of color, the accidents of slightly uneven dyeing produce variations in luminosity but, as with Gordon Hart, we are more aware of light on the work than in it. Another young artist—a painter, it is safe to say—who con-

fronts the issue of light in painting as directly as it is possible to do so is Robert Swain. His large pictures, each constituted of separate squares of stretched canvas, are "meta-color charts"; they present schematized scales of value, hue and saturation in the manner, superficially, of ordinary color charts, but without even implied reference to those or any other object. Swain's is perhaps the purest painting possible; following the example of certain Kellys (both the early square-unit series and the later color-spectrum, contiguous-panel series), Swain concentrates exclusively on the properties of color to make some of the most luminous pictures of the decade. By antithetical means, Robert Ryman also achieves an outstanding light; Ryman uses only strokes of white paint, which, in their physical absorption by the paper or cloth

Romantically luminous Minimalism: Ralph Humphrey's untitled 1969 painting, 60 inches high. Bykert Gallery, New York.

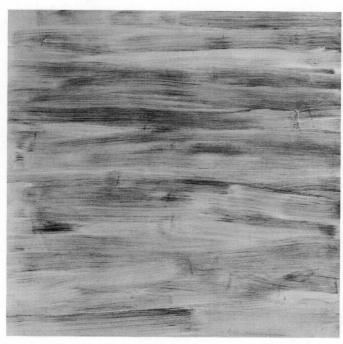

Robert Ryman's *Standard*, 1967, enamel on steel, 48 inches high. is all white, but subtly, atmospherically lit. Fischbach **gallery.**

Agnes Martin fills *The City*, 1966, 72 inches high, with uncannily atmospheric depths. Elkon Gallery, New York.

support, cause a subtly shifting and atmospheric sensation harking back to Guston, and to gestural abstraction's brushed inflections of tone. Ryman is not free of the literalism of our moment, however; eliminating stretchers in favor of stapling, glueing or taping his pictures directly onto the wall, he creates an anti-illusionist tension which contradicts the freely atmospheric play of his subdued white light. The now shiny, now mat surface further underscores Ryman's flirtation with literalism.

The only group of painters entirely unconcerned with objectness are the new realists, the figurative painters who have moved beyond French and Expressionist precedents to rediscover a clear and direct representationalism. The low-key, blurred light in a John Button cityscape, when compared to the glaring, even harsh light in a Richard Estes cityscape (full as it is of doublings, of depicted reflections) shows us how the pastoral, atmospheric sensibility and the predilection for the man-made, artificially lit urban scene are divisive even among a relatively homogenous stylistic group. The opposing styles of Guston and Reinhardt have been seen to share a preoccupation with atmospheric light; conversely, the similar styles of Button and Estes are opposed in their kinds of light—the one romantically full of weather and gentle tonal play; the other as clear, fast and urban as any Sheeler. Of the other important new realists, Philip Pearlstein, especially, has played a central role in reidentifying light with the value system while Alex Katz makes a brilliantly lit style which conjoins Matissean pure color and the "traditional" depiction of mass. They all have a common ancestor in Hopper; after one-fourth of a century of major accomplishment in abstract painting, American art seems poised on the threshold of a return to figuration, from which we may expect a variety of lights to emerge.

Is there a New York light? The common subject matter of Button and Estes would indicate that there is not, but the photographs of Rudolph Burckhardt and the blue-rose period in Guston's career both capture a phenomenon also present in "New York School" poetry, like James Schuyler's whose *February* starts: "A chimney, breathing a little smoke./ The sun, I can't see/ making a bit of pink/ I can't quite see in the blue . . ." This trinity—photo, painting, poem—is too closely related for us to deny that yes, there is, at least *one* New York light, perversely a combination of the atmospheric, landscape-like tradition and urban inspiration. Beyond that, one cannot generalize: other lights gleam from individual eyes.

By one of the most nuanced stylists of the new realism: John Button's *Blue Windows*, 1964, 52 inches high. L. Kornblee, New York.

Richard Estes' *Brownstone Reflections*, 1967, 23⅜ inches high, eliminates atmosphere for a hard, brilliant sheen. Stone Gallery, New York.

This 1948 photograph of the Flatiron Building by painter/photographer/filmmaker Rudolph Burckhardt captures something of the quality of the New York light that has inspired a generation of artists, abstract and figurative alike.

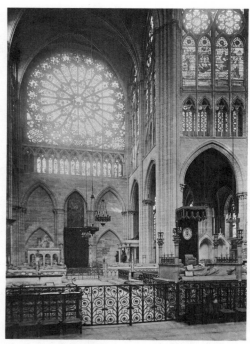

The huge rose window of the north transept of the royal abbey of St.-Denis, ca. 1245, initiated the High Gothic style, completely dissolving the upper masonry wall into delicate stone tracery filled with stained glass shedding multicolored light. The 13th-century glass, destroyed during the Revolution, is now replaced by modern panes.

Detail of 12th-century window in the choir of St.-Denis, showing Abbot Suger in obeisance at the feet of the Virgin. Suger, who directed the activities of architects, sculptors, goldsmiths and glass designers in the construction of the famous abbey, was also a minister to Louis VII.

By Florens Deuchler

Gothic Glass

The daily repeated wonder of the rising sun as bringer of light and warm life plays an important role in many cultures and religions. The sun often symbolizes the mystery of God, and revealing testimonies of this transformation still exist. In modern Greek, for instance, the expression for "sunset" is a poetic and explicit one; the Greeks say that when it goes down to the horizon and sinks into the red-colored sea, "the sun becomes king."

In the West, one nation is especially dedicated to the wonder of light: France. Hans Sedlmayr has pointed out in an apostrophic survey how the French have always been deeply impressed by the phenomenon: medieval stained-glass windows, mirrored galleries, the "Sun King," Impressionist painting, the magic in modern French films where light itself becomes an essential "actor."

The greatest contribution of France to medieval culture is the creation of the stained-glass window when it reached its full potential as a monumental art. The beginnings of this fragile art are uncertain. According to legend, glass is a Phoenician discovery and, therefore, more than 2,000 years old. As recorded in literary sources, it was often used for windows in late antiquity and early Christian times. The German monk Theophilus Presbyter in his *Schedula diversarum artium,* of the 10th or 11th century, says that the stained-glass window was a craft long practiced in France (*"quiquid in fenestrarum pretiose varietate diligit Francia"*); and the chronicle of St. Remi in Reims, dating from 905, says the windows in this church depicted various stories.

Theophilus also gives in his treatise valuable information about the early medieval formula for making glass: two parts ash of beechwood or fern, yielding potash, an alkaline base; and one part river sand, washed free of earthy particles. He explains that when the glass mixture is fused for a long

Florens Deuchler, Swiss-born art historian, is chairman of the medieval department of the Metropolitan Museum and director of The Cloisters. He has published many books, articles and scholarly editions of medieval texts; among several works to be published soon by the Metropolitan is his *The Year 1200: between Romanesque and Gothic, a Background Survey,* to appear in 1970.

time, it assumes a rather warm purplish cast, due to the presence of manganese in the ashes of the plants used. The obtained glass was colored in the mass by different metallic oxides and various other ingredients added to the molten mixture while in the process of fusion. Suger, the famous twelfth-century abbot of St. Denis, near Paris, claims to have ground up sapphires in order to obtain the blues of his panes. This obviously expensive procedure may have been wishful thinking rather than reality. It is, however, interesting and significant for the often made comparison of stained glass with precious stones; jewels were many times described as sources of light. Heinrich von Veldeke, for instance, in his great epic *Aeneid,* described stained-glass windows as "Of garnets and of sapphires,/Of emeralds and rubies,/Of chrysolites and sardons,/Topazes and beryls . . ."

In the time of Theophilus, the silhouettes of the glass pieces needed for depictions in the windows were drawn on a wooden table coated with whitewash; later on they were cut out in parchment. The pieces of glass were set upon the model and cut with a red-hot iron, the rough edges being clipped off with pliers called "grozing irons." When the glass had been assembled as required on the cartoon or actual-size working-drawing, the glazier traced the design. The elaboration of details was accomplished by covering the glass with a pigment, working the outline-drawing into it, getting rid of the highlights, and laying on lines and shadows. The pigment used had to be of a kind that could be fused in the glass oven without being destroyed. Theophilus also gives exact instructions in his treatise for this procedure.

Late in the 10th century in France, a stain was invented made of chloride of silver, which on being fired on the surface of the glass imparted a yellow or golden color. This silver stain could be directly applied to white glass to make required parts yellow as, for instance, to show yellow or golden hair not separated from the face by hard lead lines. Applied to blue glass, it could make green trees, birds and water plants bordering on blue sheets of water, so that small landscapes were executed without intervening leads.

Another innovation arose from the peculiar character of "ruby" glass. Copper, the coloring medium in this case, acts so powerfully that light could not penetrate a glass stained with it. A lump of plain white glass was therefore dipped into molten glass stained red with copper for getting a thin ruby film on the outside. As the ruby color only coats the surface of the glass, the artist can remove the colored layer and apply the stain to the white glass below, thus achieving three colors in one lead.

After the painting, the numerous pieces—350 to 450 per square meter have been counted—were again placed upon the model for mounting with leading. This work recalls the technique of the mosaic-maker. Often the drawing is done almost entirely by leading and makes one forget its techni-

cal necessity. The finished panel was finally reinforced with iron armatures and put into the window. Light shines through the panes. The air bubbles, bumps, flaws, impurities and irregularities in the glass break up the sun's rays. The vibrating, refracted light makes the walls shine. The stained-glass windows become, mysteriously, a communicating shade between God and man.

The climax of this art lies in the 13th century. Only in the past few decades have art historians become aware of the importance of the thousands and thousands of windows in French cathedrals and churches. A huge number of these paintings made with colored glass and light are lost; most

Influenced by the medallion windows of the late 12th century are the illustrated bibles with themes of the New Testament and the lives of saints and martyrs.
Below left: Detail of page from a 13th-century Moralized Bible (British Museum).
Below right: Detail of St. Lawrence Window, ca. 1170, St. Pierre Cathedral, Poitiers.

Medallion from a typical 13th-century narrative window of the so-called School of Paris: *St. Martin of Tours Sharing His Coat with a Beggar*, ca. 1275, Cathedral of St.-Gratien, at Tours.

Detail of the choir of the Cathedral of St.-Gratien, Tours, 1257-80, showing the ultimate evolution of the Gothic wall with stained glass filling the spaces between slender stone mullions.

Gothic Glass

books and already existing cartoons. The glaziers' cartoons were drawn on parchment; they could, therefore, be kept and used again as occasion permitted. The size of the window to be glazed decided the scale of the reproduction and the possibilities of adding to or subtracting from an original design. In the later Middle Ages, they often copied the *Biblia Pauperum,* a religious picture-book depicting the paramount events of the Old and New Testament. Stained-glass windows from such models, incorporating illustrations of the story of Christ, the Virgin, the apostles, martyrs and saints, are themselves a "picture-bible" for those unable to read. Suger in the 12th century and Jean Gerson at the beginning of the 15th century asserted: "The images in the church windows are put there for no other purpose than to show simple folk ignorant of the Scriptures what they ought to believe." And from an old catechism of the diocese of Tréguier, one learns that upon entering a church, the visitor has to "take holy water, adore the Blessed Sacrament, then walk all around the edifice and look at the stained-glass windows."

Beyond didactic purposes, stained-glass windows were parts of an elaborate theological program. Patriarchs, prophets and patron saints of the church were generally placed in the clerestory windows on the north side. On the south side are the apostles, martyrs and great saints of Christianity, those whose relics were owned by the church or who were especially honored in the diocese. In a prominent place in the chevet or in the west front, the Tree of Jesse can be found—a genealogy of Christ in the form of a tree rooted in Jesse's body and showing Christ's ancestors up to Mary in the branches. The link between the Old and New Testament is didactically stressed also in the narrative panes in the lower windows. These scenes fitted into medallions—circles, squares, lozenges, quatrefoils—usually read from left to right, starting at the bottom. A complete iconographic program can still be studied in Chartres where the original interrelationship of space, light and plastic effects is practically untouched. Chartres is, however only one among many Gothic monuments where the development of light, the use of which is without precedent or parallel, can be followed.

Between 1150 and 1350, the Gothic wall gradually became porous: light filtered through it, permeated it, merged with it, transfigured it. The Gothic may be described as transparent, diaphanous architecture—an esthetic principle developed with complete consistency and to its ultimate consequences. The gradual enlargement of the windows as such was not the most important manifestation of this process. No segment of inner space was allowed to remain in darkness, undefined by light. The side aisles, the galleries above them, the ambulatory and chapels of the choir, became narrower and shallower, their external walls pierced by continuous rows of windows. According to medieval thinkers, light represented the principle of order and value. It is the creative principle in all things, most active in the

of the existing windows were frequently restored or partly remade. Even Suger of St. Denis had to charge a master-specialist with the preservation of the windows. What has been preserved throughout the centuries is important enough however, to make us reconsider the history of Gothic painting and to investigate who the glazier-artist was. He certainly belonged to a highly specialized team which doubtless moved from town to town as fast as orders were received. Many hands that we find before in other places, for instance, can be distinguished in Chartres.

For their subjects and their treatment, the glaziers drew on many sources, including illuminated manuscripts, model

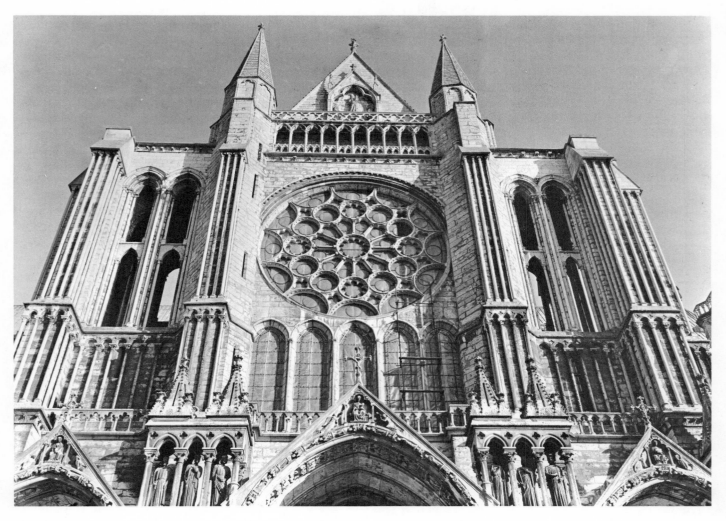

Above: South transept façade of Chartres, ca. 1210-20. **Below:** Rose of the north transept of Chartres, given by St. Louis and Queen Blanche of Castile. The glass, ca. 1230-35, is notably lighter and more luminous than the later rose windows of Paris and Reims.

heavenly spheres (whence it causes all organic growth on earth) and weakest in the earthly substances. Light is actually the mediator between bodiless and bodily substances (Robert Grosseteste), a spiritual body or, as he calls it, an embodied spirit. According to the Platonizing metaphysics of the Middle Ages, light is the most noble of natural phenomena, the least material, the closest approximation to pure form, to beauty. Such thinkers as Hugh of St. Victor and Thomas Aquinas ascribe two main characteristics to the Beautiful: consonance of parts or proportion, and luminosity. To the medieval mind beauty was not a value independent of others, but rather the radiance of truth, the splendor of ontological perfection, and that quality of things which reflects their origin in God. Light and luminous objects, no less than musical consonance, conveyed an insight into the perfection of the cosmos and a divination of the Creator. Therefore the stars, gold and precious stones are called beautiful because of this quality, and in the philosophical literature of the time, as in the courtly epic, no attributes are used more frequently to describe visual beauty than "lucid," "luminous," "clear."

Abbot Suger of St. Denis, who built a new abbey church in the 1140s—the first one in the upcoming Gothic style—

described and interpreted his church and its art treasures in two separate treatises: the "Booklet on the Consecration of the Church of St. Denis" deals entirely with it and stresses the esthetic value of harmony, recalling the actual building. His "Report on the Administration" describes the complete monument. In the *"caput"* or chevet of his church, Suger erected a remarkable stained-glass window. Illustrating a passage in Chapter XI of the Book of the Prophet Isaiah, this window helps to understand the character of the new art created at St. Denis. Suger's church is itself the mystical image of heaven: *"Bright is the noble edifice that is pervaded by the new light."* Lux nova refers also to Christ and therefore to the symbolic or "anagogical" significance of the physical light. In the case of Suger's choir at St. Denis, the substitution of a bright church for a dark one was one

of the most striking features *("ut . . . ex tenebrosiore splendidam redderent ecclesiam")*.

We learn about Abbot Suger's theory of light from his theological statements. Based upon the Neo-Platonic philosophy attributed to Dionysius the Areopagite (who has erroneously been identified with the patron saint of the abbey), this theory argued that man could come to a closer understanding of the light of God through the light of material objects in the physical world. This accounts for Suger's interest not only in magnificent liturgical vessels of gold and silver, but also for the extraordinary set of stained glass windows with which he adorned the radiating chapels of the chevet of St. Denis. He understood that stained glass had three basic properties: it was a bearer of holy images, an intrinsically rich material resembling precious stones, and

Above: Nave and apse of the Benedictine Abbey of Ste.-Foy de Conques, built 1030-65. The austere Romanesque interior is meagerly illuminated by small windows piercing the thick walls.

Left: Choir of the Cathedral of Sées, late 13th century. The open triforium seems to prolong the upper windows, an airy effect heightened by the slender piers rising to meet the rib-vaulting.

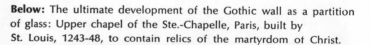

Below: The ultimate development of the Gothic wall as a partition of glass: Upper chapel of the Ste.-Chapelle, Paris, built by St. Louis, 1243-48, to contain relics of the martyrdom of Christ.

The Tree of Jesse window at St.-Denis—one of the oldest in the royal abbey—dates from the 12th century. It exemplifies Suger's innovating story-telling themes.

How closely related miniature painting was to glass can be seen in *The Tree of Jesse*, page from the Ingeborg Psalter, painted in the eastern Ile-de-France, ca. 1195. Musée Condé, Chantilly.

a mystery, because it glowed without fire, and without heat. Luminosity is for the Gothic eye a feature demanded and singled out for praise by contemporaries—not only for its esthetic aspect but also for its symbolic one. The stained-glass windows, through which the clarity of the sun is transmitted according to Pierre Roissy (Chancellor of the See in Chartres and head of a famous theological school about 1200), also manifest the Holy Texts, and they therefore repel evil and illuminate us.

Bibliographical Note

The best survey is to be found in: Otto von Simson, *The Gothic Cathedral, Origins of Gothic Architecture and the Medieval Concept of Order.* New York, 1962. For the problems of light see also: Hans Sedlmayr, *Die Entstehung der Kathedrale,* Zurich, 1950. The interrelationship between stained-glass windows and illuminated manuscripts is dealt with in: Florens Deuchler, *Der Ingeborgpsalter,* Berlin, 1967. For all stained-glass problems see the many important contributions by Louis Grodecki. For a bibliography of this great French scholar, see F. Deuchler, op. cit. A complete catalogue of all extant examples of medieval stained glass throughout the world is the goal of the *Corpus Vitrearum Medii Aevi.* The *Corpus* will include approximately 80 volumes. One of this series has been designated to include the medieval stained glass in American museums and collections. Patronage of the undertaking has been accorded by the Union Internationale Académique, the American Council of Learned Societies and UNESCO.

Close to the French High Gothic style is the apse of Leon Cathedral, Spain, ca. 1225,
with stained glass windows dating from the late 13th-early 14th centuries.

The Risen Christ as Apollo
ascending in a chariot;
3rd-century mosaic on a vault
in the necropolis under the
Basilica of St. Peter's, Rome.

The Adoration of the Magi (detail) as a Roman imperial
audience; 5th-century mosaic on the triumphal
arch in the nave of Sta. Maria Maggiore, Rome.

*The Virgin Presenting the Child
to the World;* 9th century, gold-
background mosaic half-dome,
Church of the Assumption,
Nicaea (destroyed in 1922)

By John Beckwith

Byzantium: Gold and Light

"And how comes gold to be a beautiful thing? And lightning by night and stars, why are these so fair?" Plotinus.

The earliest Christian vault and wall mosaics so far discovered are in a small mausoleum not far from the tomb of St. Peter on the Vatican hill. The mausoleum was built towards the end of the 2nd century for the Julii family but the mosaics probably date from the middle of the 3rd century. In the center of the vault against a gold ground, a beardless charioteer dressed in a tunic and a flying cloak, nimbed with rays shooting upwards and sideways like the arms of a cross, bearing in the left hand an orb, the right (now missing) probably raised in an act of benediction, represents the risen and ascending Christ, the new *Sol Invictus, Sol Salutis, Sol Iustitiae*. The pagan type of the sun-god in his chariot, or the apotheosis of an emperor or a hero, has been adapted to the Christian belief in the risen God, His triumph over death, and through the orb in His left hand, His eternal dominion. Solar similes including that of the sunrise had been applied to innumerable pharaohs and to the great kings of Persia. In the course of time not only the Roman emperors but most of the gods were identified in one way or another with the sun. Mithras was a god of the morning light. The language of many books of the Old Testament is rich in solar metaphors: the Sun of Righteousness, the Sun of Justice. The rising sun was linked with the Advent of Christ and the Feasts of Christmas and Epiphany —the latter was the "Feast of Lights." The *troparion* sung on Christmas Day included the words "Thou hast risen, Christ, from the Virgin, thou intelligible Sun of Righteousness." Philo, Clement of Alexandria and Origen were all familiar with this type of metaphor; Origen suggested that the faithful should turn in prayer to the East where the Sun of Righteousness ever rises and where the True Light is born.

When the Church finally triumphed in the early 4th century and Constantine lavished the full weight of imperial patronage on the building of churches in Rome, Jerusalem and Constantinople, the tangible and visual results were felt and seen through gold — from time immemorial the most precious and immutable of metals. The shrine of the Apostle Peter in Rome was of gold and precious marbles, the apse of the basilica was decorated with gold mosaic. There was a great cross of solid gold, and the altar was silver-gilt with 400 precious stones. There was a large golden dish for the offertory, and a jeweled tower—possibly a tabernacle to house the Sacrament—with a dove of pure gold brooding over it. Before the tomb of the Apostle was a great golden corona of lights. The nave of St. Peter's was lit by 32 hanging candelabra of silver and the aisles by 30 more. St. Peter's was one of the great shrines of Christendom, but its furnishings were no doubt rivaled by the decoration of the basilicas and martyria built by Constantine in the eastern provinces of the Empire.

At Salonika in the rotunda now known as Hagios Giorgios, Early Christian art visibly soars from the arcosolium of the private tomb to the domes of an imperial palace. The building was almost certainly part of the palace built by Theodosius I towards the end of the 4th century. The dome is richly decorated with mosaic. Against a gold ground, in front of imposing architectural fantasies, ecclesiastic, military and civilian saints stand in prayer, dressed in splendor, unnaturally beautiful in form and face, recalling no doubt the gesturing Augusti in a hall of state. In the years of its triumph, the Church turned naturally to the ceremonial of the imperial court for the symbolic expression of divine authority and power. For numbers of years the monarchy had been "sacred," its statutes "celestial"; the people adored "Our Serenity" and the Sacred Purple. Now in "all the loveliness of color and the light of the sun," to adapt Plotinus, the mosaics of Hagios Giorgios express the glory of *Roma aeterna* in a new Christian guise and pay homage to Christ Who is the true founder of the Holy City. Color is conceived as light materialized; color emphasizes "the conquest of darkness inherent in matter by the pouring in of

John Beckwith is deputy keeper of the department of architecture and sculpture at the Victoria and Albert Museum, London. He is the author of a standard introduction to Byzantine art, *The Art of Constantinople* (Praeger), and has been guest lecturer at many universities and museums in England and America.

The Archangel Michael, silver-gilt and enameled icon,
10th century, among the objects looted from Constantinople
during the 4th Crusade. Treasury of St. Mark's, Venice.

St. Porphyrios, late 4th-century mosaic, o‹
of a series of heroic saints on the vault
of the church of Hagios Giorgios, Saloni›

light, the unembodied" (Plotinus). Gold and light provided the firmament beneath which the divine and imperial liturgies could be enacted like a sacred drama.

After the Council of Ephesus (431) had declared the Virgin Mary to be Theotokos, the Mother of God, Pope Sixtus III (432-440) built the great basilica in Rome to Sta. Maria Maggiore and adorned the church with mosaics. On the triumphal arch, imperial iconography is again evident. In scenes depicting the childhood of Christ, the Virgin is dressed as an Augusta and the Adoration of the Magi is interpreted in the terms of an imperial audience. Later the Byzantine Church was to object to the representation of the Virgin decked with the trappings of earthly majesty mainly on the grounds that it was unseemly for the natural and supernatural orders to be so closely synthesized. Nevertheless, Emperor Leo VI the Wise (889-912) was to state categorically in a sermon delivered in Hagia Sophia early in his reign that the Virgin was glorified by the light she had given to the world. The light was none other than Christ Himself, Who is Divine Wisdom. The Virgin as Mother of an Emperor is herself an Empress, and to her Leo owes everything he possesses, especially his empire, and he implores her to protect and guide him. In the mosaic over the imperial doorway of Hagia Sophia, Leo the Wise makes *proskynesis* before Christ Who is Wisdom, Light and Peace, while the Archangel Gabriel and the Virgin, Messenger and Instrument of the Incarnation, make constant intercession for him who is Christ's Vicar on earth.

When Justinian's great church dedicated to Holy Wisdom was completed in 537, informed opinion considered it to be technically daring, perfect in harmony, "marvelous and terrifying." Procopius stated that "it was singularly full of light and sunshine; you would declare that the place is not lighted by the sun from without, but that the rays are produced

The Transfiguration, ca. 550, mosaic in apse of the church in St. Catherine's Monastery, Mt. Sinai. Intact since Justinian's day, it is probably the work of mosaicists from Constantinople.

The Virgin Orans, 1043-46, gold background mosaic,
apse of the Cathedral of St. Sophia, Kiev.

within itself, such an abundance of light is poured into this church." Further on in his panegyric he remarks "from the lightness of the building it does not appear to rest on a solid foundation, but to cover the place beneath as though it were suspended from heaven by the fabled golden chain . . . The entire ceiling is covered with pure gold, which adds glory to its beauty, though the rays of light reflected upon the gold from the marble surpass it in beauty . . . Whoever enters there to worship perceives at once that it is not by any human strength or skill, but by the favor of God that this work has been perfected; his mind rises sublime to commune with God, feeling that He cannot

be far off, but must especially love to dwell in the place which He has chosen; and this takes place not only when a man sees it for the first time, but it always makes the impression on him, as though he had never beheld it before." Hagia Sophia was a court church. The vast central space, enveloped by the huge dome and semi-domes, was reserved for the clergy of the Patriarch and for the Emperor and his retinue. The Empress and her suite sat in the gallery at the west end facing the distant altar. The public—and one wonders how many of the common people were admitted in the 6th century—were confined to some of the aisles and galleries. Hagia Sophia was the largest and most

Apse of the Cathedral of Cefalù, ca. 1150, showing Christ holding
the Gospel Book opened to the text "I am the light of the World."

expensive religious theater imaginable, built and furnished for the semi-private performances of the divine and imperial liturgy. The audience was God.

Hagia Sophia was on the whole devoid of figurated mosaics, possibly for iconoclastic reasons, but more likely on technical grounds; the church was too big for figures in mosaic to register. We may be sure that other churches at Constantinople were not so severely planned. There can be little reason to doubt that the team of mosaicists who decorated the church in St. Catherine's monastery on Mount Sinai were sent from the metropolis, and that on Mount Sinai is preserved the only example of pure Byzantine style

in mosaic dating from the middle of the century. By a happy coincidence the dominating scene in the apse is the Transfiguration. Christ is represented between Elias and Moses, a theophany shimmering in white, gold and silver framed by a mandorla in shades of blue from which emerge broad rays of silver light. Below this awe-inspiring apparition the Apostles John and James kneel and gesture in astonishment and acclamation; St. Peter sprawls beneath the feet of Christ. Light, the unembodied, has transfigured the Son of Man. Similarly, in the imperial portraits of San Vitale at Ravenna, gold—color conceived as light materialized—and light itself evoke at the same time the natural

Christ Pantocrator, ca. 1100, gold-background mosaic in the dome of the Church of the Dormition, Daphni.

The Virgin and Child Enthroned between Emperors Constantine I and Justinian I, mosaic tympanum, ca. 1000, Hagia Sophia, Istanbul.

The Virgin and Child between Emperor John Comnenus and the Empress Irene, mosaic panel, ca. 1118, Hagia Sophia, Istanbul.

The Emperor Leo VI, the Wise, prostrated before Christ, 886-912, mosaic over the western door of Hagia Sophia, Istanbul.

and the supernatural image. Justinian, the Vicar of God, is the imperial ideal incarnate. The imperial epiphany is revealed before a gold background on a green floor; to prevent the nimbus behind the Emperor's head from merging into the gold ground, the artists outlined it in sharply defined red with an additional contour of silver. There is no attempt to suggest place. The finite forms, the attributes of power, the portraits from life, all suggest a moment of time when the slightly swaying movement of a slow procession has suddenly turned as one man to confront the spectator. In this act of slightly swaying, suddenly turning, all members of the imperial cortege bend their proud, stern yet kindly gaze on the subject faithful. At the same time this vision emerges from and radiates light, color and harmony in a golden infinity.

This timeless aspect of Divinity is evoked more than once in Byzantine mosaic. The mosaic in the apse of the Church of the Dormition at Nicaea, which had been restored in the 9th century after the Iconoclast Controversy by a certain Naukratios, revealed the Virgin against a gold ground standing on a dais and presenting the Child to the world. Above her head a hand emerged from heaven and three rays of silver light through which an inscription read: "Thou hast conceived Him before Time." The hand of God and the three rays represent the Trinity, the procession of the Son from the hand of the Father, the Logos, which existed before Time, and the divine origin of the Child made flesh by the consent of the Virgin. The words of the inscription repeat the first words of a hymn sung during the office for the feast of the Triumph of Orthodoxy celebrated on the first Sunday in Lent. No Byzantine mosaic gives better evidence of the lofty theological atmosphere in which the first works of church decoration were undertaken after the end of the Controversy, and the destruction of the church of the Dormition at Nicaea must be regarded as one of the major artistic losses of modern times. Again, the mosaic on the tympanum in the south-west vestibule of Hagia Sophia presents the Virgin and Child enthroned between the Emperors Constantine I and Justinian I. It has been suggested that the decoration was ordered to commemorate the victory of the usurping Emperor John I Tzimisces (969-976) over Svjatoslav, Prince of Kiev, in 971, which was attributed to the parading of an icon of the Theotokos Hodegetria before the Byzantine army or, alternatively, to celebrate the victories of Basil II which culminated in his triumph over the Bulgars in 1017. On the other hand, the victories are in a sense irrelevant. The founder of Constantinople is offering the city and the builder of the greatest church in Christendom is offering Hagia Sophia to the Virgin and at any time it would only be right and

Right: Over the vast central space of Hagia Sophia, the huge dome seems miraculously suspended in the light of its myriad windows. The church was erected in 532-37 by Justinian I.

The Angel and the Virgin face each other at right angles in *The Annunciation* set in a squinch of the Church of the Dormition, Daphni, ca. 1100.

fitting for these Emperors to be so signally commemorated in a place of honor. They are dressed in medieval imperial regalia, the emphasis being on the gold *stemma,* the stiff, jeweled *loros,* and the scarlet buskins studded with pearls, but the gold ground against which they are set, the still forms of the Virgin and Child looking past the Emperors down into the vestibule, and the plain foreground all stress the infinite rather than a moment of time.

The Comnene portraits in the same church represent the Emperor John II Comnenus holding a bag of gold and the Empress Irene holding a diploma; they stand on either side of the Virgin who is also standing. The panel was presumably set up to commemorate their accession in 1118. The portrait of the prince Alexius was probably added nearby in 1122, when he was proclaimed co-Emperor at the age of 17. We are confronted by a state portrait at a given moment of time: the swarthy Emperor with his long

nose and steadfast expression, the high moral principles of his public and private life made fact by his very presence, the devout Irene with her fair hair and clear complexion, and the sickly Caesar, ill-tempered and rather petulant. We are reminded of the court ceremony of the Rise of the Despot—*Anatolé tou Despotou* (the Greek word *Anatolé* means sunrise as well as the East)—amid the chants:

Faction-leaders: "Rise, God-possessed kingship."
People: "Rise, rise, rise."
F.L. "Rise, John and Alexius, autocrats of the Romans."
P. "Rise, rise, rise."
F.L. "Rise, servants of the Lord."
P. "Rise, rise, rise."
F.L. "Rise, Irene, Augusta of the Romans."
P. "Rise, rise, rise." And so on.

The ceremony took place in the Hippodrome as the Augusti mounted the stairs to the imperial box before being revealed to the people. Sometimes, it would take place in a public square on a special stage hung with gold curtains which at the end of the chants were drawn to one side, unveiling the Augusti as it were. On the other hand, the presence of the Virgin and Child in the Comnene portrait, with their grave, gentle and alert expressions, the drapery sensitively modeled and naturalistically treated, postulate the true reality between the bedizened images of earthly power.

Emphasis on light and color gave a particular significance to optical theory and experiment. In Hagia Sophia, at Hosios Loukas and at Daphni there are optical devices to increase the quantity of light within the mosaic, aided of course by the squinches, pendentives and curved surfaces. Even on plain surfaces the setting bed was never flat. The catholicon at Daphni is dominated by one of the most tremendous visions of Christ Pantocrator ever conceived by man. Against a glittering gold ground Christ is revealed in the aspect of Jehovah, a heavy Semitic judge with thick nose and full, cruel mouth, the thick-browed eyes gazing pitilessly to one side, the lower lids underlined with shadow, the long hair offset by a full beard and mustache, the massive shoulders clothed in a brown-gold tunic and a dark blue cloak, one sinewy hand grasping a jeweled codex, the other raised in blessing, but conveying also menace and condemnation. Elsewhere in the church all is light and grace. The Annunciation, for example, is set in a squinch; the Angel and the Virgin are at right angles to one another. The Angel in classical dress walks with a gesture of salutation towards the Virgin, who is seated on a cushioned stool. There is nothing between them but a gold void which frames and projects them before the spectator. The vividness of the colors, the attention to detail in a firmament of gold, the sharp sense of form and gesture, the fresh wind of classicism, make the mosaics of Daphni a turning point from the somber records of theophany in the Nea Moni on Chios, or at Kiev, the old hieratic feasts of the Church, or the grim presence of countless saints. At Daphni there is an atmosphere of joy as though the Byzantine heart had ceased to brood over the sorrows of God and Man and had lifted to the call of angels.

All visitors to Constantinople could not fail to be astonished by the innumerable miracles of the goldsmith's art to be found there. The sheer massing of gold ornament in the churches of the city, even if the ordinary folk never penetrated further than the outer courts of the Sacred Palace, were enough to confirm the impression of boundless wealth, mastery over the world and endless favor to the God-guarded city. The 30 gold crowns hanging before the altar of Hagia Sophia are no more, and all that survives of such ornament is a fragment of a small votive crown of the Emperor Leo VI in gold and enamel, bearing his portrait, now in the treasury of San Marco, Venice. More characteristic of the type of ornament to be found in Byzantine churches is the superb icon of the Archangel Michael in the same treasury, an evocation of angelic majesty

in which gold plays the major part and the gold filigree, the little enameled busts of saints and the precious stones are merely lavish trimmings. The great reliquary at Limburg, silver-gilt, enameled, set with pearls and precious stones, was designed for a relic of the True Cross, fragments of the clothing of Christ and the Virgin, the Sponge, fragments of the Crown of Thorns, and the hair of St. John the Baptist. The True Cross had been mounted in a setting of pearls and precious stones at the command of the Emperor Constantine VII Porphyrogenitus and his son Romanus. The remainder had been set in their rich case on the order of Basil the Proedros (President of the Council), a bastard of the Emperor Romanus I Lacapenus and a eunuch, one of the leading figures of the court, an able general and a gifted statesman. Items such as this would be paraded during the great feasts of the Church, accompanied by lights and incense, or placed in state on a golden throne. Above all, the Pala d'Oro in San Marco, in size alone and for all

Votive crown of the Emperor Leo VI, gold and enamel, late 9th or early 10th century. Treasury of St. Mark's, Venice.

Byzantium: Gold and Light

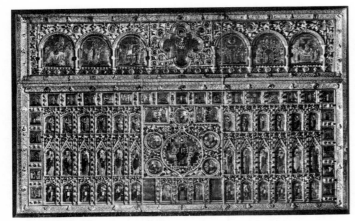

its Gothic setting, conveys to us today something of the majestic splendor of the ornament of a Byzantine church.

Unfortunately Byzantine art may never be seen as it was meant to be seen—a totality of religious and aesthetic experience. The Augusti, the court, the imperial and patriarchal processions, the hymns and chants, the great diadems and robes, the high cosmetics and the heavy scents, the multiplicity of races, the great dromons breathing Greek fire, the imperial barge glittering with gold and purple, the eunuchs, secretaries, generals, admirals in the different costume of their rank are now no more than a golden dream on a summer's day.

Above, detail below: Pala d'Oro altar front, 10th-14th century, 136½ inches wide, composed of 137 enamels set in silver-gilt with pearls and precious stones. St. Mark's Treasury, Venice.

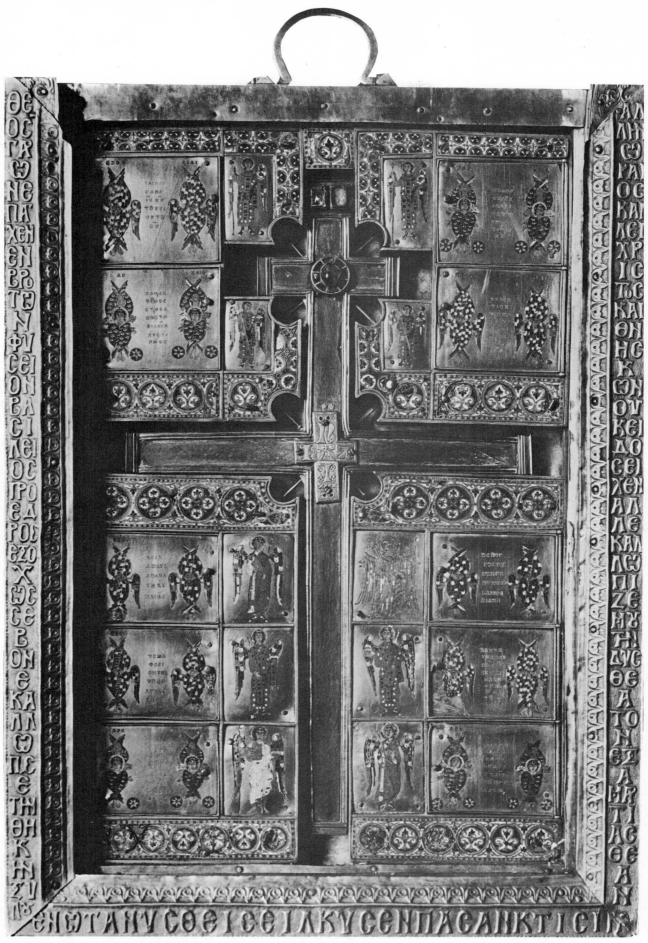

Enameled silver-gilt reliquary for a piece of the True Cross, 964-65,
interior of case, 18¾ inches high. Cathedral Treasury, Limburg-an-der-Lahn.

The plein-air painter fully accoutred:
Corot at Ville d'Avray.

Daumier: *Landscape Painters at Work.*

Photograph of
Boudin painting at Deauville.

By Gabriel Laderman

The Outer Light

The 19th century was the century of landscape painting, and the century of a new kind of landscape painting, plein-air. Some painting was even concocted in the studio aiming at the look of plein-air painting. Even those 19th-century painters, such as Caspar David Friedrich and his friend Carl Gustav Carus, and Thomas Cole and Asher Durand of the Hudson River School, who painted in the studio, made many intense and detailed drawings and sketches directly from nature as part of their general practice. More important than this, the concept behind their studio paintings came from the confrontation between the artist and nature.

Nothing in the oeuvre of major 18th-century artists or styles prepares us for the quality, character and importance of 19th century plein-air painting. During most of the 18th century, landscape painting was practiced either for its topographical value (although such artists as Canaletto and Guardi rose far above this aim) or as part of the Rococo taste, as in the works of Watteau and Gainsborough, which, for all their greatness, are as like the reality of landscape as the French court's shepherds and milkmaids were like the real thing. Surprisingly it was from England, where only portrait painting had flourished, that much of the impetus for 19th-century landscape painting came.

Eighteenth-century England produced a group of inspired amateur estheticians and critics unhampered by academic orthodoxies. The most important were Edmund Burke, Archibald Allison, William Gilpin, Richard Payne Knight and Uvedale Price. Burke's essay on "The Sublime and the Beautiful" was an early attempt to understand the aims and actions of art in terms of abstract qualities. Literary subject matter, classical allusion—whether Virgilian or Homeric—and the formal simplification of Greek and Roman masters were all discarded as a basis for the qualities arrived at and the emotions induced by art. Burke's description of the Sublime was particularly original. He believed that in art indistinctness through lack of light, representations of enormous

Gabriel Laderman, himself a well-known plein-air landscape painter, shows at the Schoelkopf Gallery and teaches painting and drawing at Queens College, New York.

depth, vertical movement continuing above the edge of the canvas, or a sense of enormous expanse extending beyond the canvas to the left or right would create in the viewer's mind a momentary awareness of his own insignificance and that the ensuing terror would be translated into identification with the image and a consequent experience of exaltation, when the viewer once more became aware that he was merely looking at a painting. Burke's definition of the Sublime seemed to later English critics to have left out the qualities they appreciated in Ruysdael, Hobbema and more particularly in rustic nature. For these qualities, William Gilpin coined the term Picturesque, which he described as all that was irregular and rough in nature. In harmony with his taste for the Picturesque in nature, in art Gilpin preferred the first sketch, rough and summary, true to the artist's first perception. Price codified the idea of the Picturesque further and applied it to landscape gardening. The new garden architecture aimed at a roughness and naturalness, the look of nature improved by conforming it to pictorial rules, instead of the formal patterns of earlier, "French" gardens. The *jardin anglais* swept the Continent in the late 18th and early 19th century. This new taste included a preference for the look of a peasant's cottage and the ruin, not because of their associations with Rousseau or with the classical past, but because they were made up of picturesque forms, that is, irregular and rough ones. Allison and Knight, who denied the specific associations which Burke, Price and Kant accepted as intrinsic to certain forms and compositions, held instead that what the associations were would depend on the previous experience of the viewer. Knight held that the only visual quality which was inherent and not associational was that of color (an amazing prophecy of the character of late 19th-century plein-air painting). This philosophical position placed in the hands of the artist the responsibility through his choice of composition, technique and color for the emotions expressed by his work. Artists of Romantic sensibility clamoring for arenas open enough to allow their emotions free play were thus directed to landscape painting.

The paintings of Friedrich and Carus were close to literal translation of the ideas of Kant and Burke into paint. Friedrich's most successful paintings depend on the conscious use, separately and commingled, of those qualities isolated by Burke as typical of the Sublime, such as the continuation of the horizontal beyond the edge of the canvas, enormous interior spaces, continuation of the vertical above the upper edge of the canvas and obscurity produced by fog and darkness. There was also a sense, as expressed by the painter Philip Otto Runge in 1802, and by Courbet later on in the century, that past art was closed, that the old forms were dead in all their perfection, and that the new artists must approach nature directly with the utmost naïveté in order to arrive at work of any quality or relevance.

While it is true that the Neo-Classic landscape tradition in France had become increasingly dry and generalized, the school of Valenciennes, Michallon and the elder Bertin (the major Neo-Classic landscape painters) did in fact produce Corot. Valenciennes, in his drawing book, recommended radical changes in the Neo-Classic formulas for pictorial composition, which are reflected in Corot's work. He re-

jected the use of the *repoussoir*, that dark mass in the foreground which he felt established too arbitrarily the first plane in the spatial progression. He also preferred more natural arrangements of lights and darks rather than strict alternating bands of increasing contrast. The classicists' emphasis on the relationship of observed values and shapes to a pictorial structure dependent on constant awareness of the picture plane had a lasting influence on Corot.

Many of the great periods in the history of landscape represent moments when the city-dweller feels most intensely the loss of landscape, the beauty and purity of the rural world which he has forsaken. Landscape painting fulfills a need which is now newly felt. Such was the case in China during the Sung dynasty, and in Rome during the height of the empire—the Odyssey landscapes as well as others less famous brought the wilderness of Homeric times to the imperial city-dweller. The cities, fed by the new converts from

Watteau: *The Minuet in a Pavilion*,
21¾ inches high. Cleveland Museum.

Fragonard: *The Avenue*, 10½ inches high.
Bowes Museum, Barnard Castle, England.

The 19th-century landscapists who painted outdoors, such as Diaz, Corot, Manet and Renoir, appreciated anew the studio-concocted *fêtes champêtres* of 18th-century painters like Fragonard and Watteau, but now the colors invented by the Rococo artists were actually perceived in nature.

Poussin: *Landscape with St. Matthew*, after 1643,
39 inches high. Staatliche Museen, West Berlin.

Corot: *The Mantes Bridge,* ca. 1870,
15¼ inches high. Louvre, Paris.

The series of spatial planes in the Poussin, partly derived
from his study of sarcophagi, are still present in **Corot, but the
convention is used playfully and with the utmost freedom.**

Narcisse Diaz: *Forest at Fontainebleau,* 16 inches high.
Heckscher Museum (A. Heckscher Coll.), Huntington, N.Y.

rural life (they became the proletariat of the Industrial Revolution) and by trade from ventures all over the world, in-
creased in size at an alarming rate. The city-dwellers became perforce more and more cut off from landscape.

The new landscape painting, licensed by 18th-century
esthetic theory, influenced by ideas of the Picturesque and
of Romanticism, was also motivated by the urban resident's
desire to recapture and re-experience the wilderness.

Constable was so sure of the overwhelming rightness of
his experience in sketching that in the compositions he
painted in the studio, he invented methods for giving these
large-scale works the character and quality of his sketches,
even as they acquired greater finish and conventional ac-
ceptability. It was one of these studio productions, *The Hay
Wain,* which took Paris by storm in 1825. The flickering
irregular lights in the foliage, the directness of the brush-
work, the absence of finish by contemporary French standards and the plein-air character of the color even in studio
paintings had an overwhelming effect on radical French
painting—even though Constable's studio pictures were
tame compared to his unexhibited sketches. The clarity of
his values and the believability of his light and air astounded
contemporaries. He eschewed the brown foreground of the
Picturesque painters and the black darks of the Neo-Classi-
cists. If he used brown or black he dropped out middle
values so that the darks acted as hues against his lights to
produce a sense of emitted illumination. The cool colors in
his distances were not arbitrary. Every value and hue seem
observed. It is important to realize that the example of Constable's sketches was unknown to early 19th-century landscape painters (as was Corot and his sketches). Constable's
only lasting influence was on the Barbizon school.

The most important influence of Corot at first was on the
work of Daubigny. The two painted together and seem to

Daubigny: *In the Woods*, 1873, 9 inches high. Sterling and Francine Clark Art Institute, Williamstown, Mass.

Pissarro: *The Hermitage Road, Pontoise*, 1874, 18⅛ inches high. Private collection.

The Outer Light

have reinforced in each other the search for those most transitory hues as well as the value changes which occur as the artist paints from nature. Daubigny's sketches, the first paintings to be called in opprobrium "impressions," were the works which before the advent of Impressionism most clearly expressed the effect of light on the hues of forms in nature. Avoiding the conceptual excesses of the later Turner, Daubigny in his sketches began more and more to depend on an appreciation of the coolness and blueness of shadows in the absence of light and the warmth, yellowness and redness of the lights. In this he was joined by Boudin who, unlike Daubigny or Corot, painted plein-air paintings exclusively. He produced no studio compositions after his sketches and in his work began to translate value-change into hue-change so that the character of the light was experienced through the changing hues its presence or absence produced, as well as through value change. His friend and companion, Jongkind, although he worked up his watercolors in the studio, aimed for even more intense sensations of light, air and immediacy than in the sketch, and even in his etchings produced a violent illumination.

Considering the importance of color in painting since the early 19th century, it is incredible to realize that almost no original color theories had been formulated since the Renaissance. Reading the writings of artists, the recipe books and drawing books until that time, we almost always find stuck on at the end of a discussion of structural procedures in painting the phrase, "Color gives charm to the work." It is the last and least element to be considered. Some prejudices now and then against adjacent placement of analagous colors are expressed, but Mengs, writing in the late 18th century, was the first artist to try seriously to develop a new theory for the construction of forms in light through color. The color wheel itself was not invented until the late 18th century.

Painting out-of-doors in front of nature, the landscape painters of the 19th century worked out of a pantheistic gestalt, a blend of Sublime with other Romantic concepts. This was responsible for the character of their compositions which tended more and more to treat all parts of the painting contextually and as of equal importance. A figure was a shape and a spot of color was a nodule of light. Corot used the little figure of the boatman in the red cap in *The Bridge at Mantes* as a spatial and structural device to drop the eye into a little pool of space and begin a metaphoric development of space consistent throughout the entire painting. The

Monet: *The Four Poplars*, 1891, 32¼ inches high.
Metropolitan Museum, New York; Havemeyer Collection.

Cézanne: *View of the Arc Valley*, ca. 1885-87,
31⅞ inches high. Carnegie Institute, Pittsburgh.

The plein-air sketch, purposefully uncomposed, but influenced by
the esthetic theory of the Sublime in its arrangement, leads to Cézanne's
subtle spatial development and beyond to 20th-century abstraction.

little figure can't possibly be thought of as a subject pretext
for the painting, nor can it be looked at separately from its
context; its scale places it in depth but its color recalls it to
the surface. In this painting, a series of trees in the foreground relating to the near riverbank, which moves at a
small diagonal to the horizontal of the picture plane, forms
a screen through which we look at the river, its further bank
and two bridges which are seen through one another. The
eye, attempting to travel through space, is at first constantly
returned to the picture plane with which the near screen of
trees is identified. Forms and lines in the distance are constantly picked up by tree-trunks and branches in the foreground. The deepest point in space, the house in the upper
left-hand quadrant, is gifted with the greatest contrast between lights and cast shadows in the entire painting, and
again, despite the absence of nearby forms identified with
the picture plane, returns us to the surface. As the eye
passes down the canvas, the two bridges continue into the
forms of a stump in the foreground. The constant and consistent development of the painting through spatial ambiguities, shifting pockets of space which return the eye to the
surface, prefigures the interdependence of surface and space-
developing brushstroke in Cézanne. The incredible refine-

ment of spatial sensibility evident in this painting and in
those of other Barbizon and pre-Impressionist masters was
accompanied by an equal sensitivity to the transitory and
infinitesimal color changes in nature. In paintings wherein
so much of the quality and character of the work depended
on the sensibility of the artist and his choice of form, shape
or tone, sensitivity to hue became of the utmost importance.
In a landscape by Poussin the color and intensity of the
clothing worn by one of the figures was less important to
the ultimate pictorial structure than the red cap on the
figure in Corot's *Bridge at Mantes*. Contextual painting,
rather than landscape painting at the service of a literary subject with figure groupings, requires an intensity of observation and awareness of the changing forms in nature and on
the canvas of a different order than that in earlier painting.
Curiously enough, together with this new hypersensitivity
there came, particularly in the work of Diaz, Corot, Manet
and later Renoir, a renewed appreciation for the studio-concocted *fêtes champêtres* of Watteau and Fragonard, but
now the colors invented by the Rococo artists were perceived in nature.

Even the most technically conservative landscape painters
were affected by the process of painting and studying from

Caspar David Friedrich: *Meadows near Greifswald.*
ca. 1825, 13¾ inches high. Kunsthalle, Hamburg.

Courbet: *Low Tide,* 1865-66, 17½ inches high.
Nelson Gallery of Art, Kansas City, Mo.

The Sublime: Friedrich implies an enormous
contrast in scale between nature and man;
Courbet emphasizes the immediacy of the experience.

Pierre-Henry de Valenciennes: *At the Villa Farnese: Buildings
Surrounded by Trees,* ca. 1786, 11½ inches high. Louvre, Paris.

Corot: *The Basilica of Constantine,* 1826-27,
9½ inches high. Private collection, Luton, England.

In his plein-air sketches of Roman scenery (though not in his studio landscapes), Valenciennes departed from the Neo-Classic tradition with its formal compositions and its alternating areas of light and dark; the resulting spontaneity directly influenced Corot's early, Italian period.

nature. Thomas Cole, in his early studies (while he still lived in Pittsburgh), decided emphatically that the outline of the forms should be arrived at only through a slow development of the interior, this in total disregard of Ingres' dictum that "line is the probity of art." The palette knife of Courbet, which he used to develop the volumes and spaces implicit in the shapes before them, became itself in many of his paintings a normative mark which defined small planes traveling through space and united the painting into an object of unified texture. He was one of the major influences on the Impressionists and his example profoundly affected the character of the brushstroke and the use to which it was put in the work of Cézanne, Pissarro and Monet.

Impressionism as a movement was unique in the history of art up to its time. The artists did not set out to be revolutionaries and their work progressed away from the example set by the Barbizon masters with slow and deliberate speed. They early accepted as axiomatic what had been the most radical portion of the artistic practice of their predecessors, the necessity of always painting from the model. The examples of Boudin, the first axiomatic plein-air painter; Jongkind, who intensified the effects of light in his studio rather than watering down the sketch; Corot, in the clarity of his light and values; Daubigny, for the organic character of his stroke in his sketches and his truth to the light of a particular moment, were not quickly out-distanced by the younger Impressionists. They adhered to the constant practice of plein-air painting with increasing tenacity. This forced the artists to concentrate on development of style as an outgrowth of the character of their procedure. Cézanne, for instance, strove for monumentality from the beginning. He

attempted with mixed success, beginning with the influence of Courbet and Zurbarán, to work towards the sort of monumentality expressed in Giotto or Masaccio. The influence of Pissarro's practice and example in the procedure of plein-air painting, the consequent shortening of his stroke to deal with foliage in patterns of light and dark, the necessity for working through the forms of the outdoors bit by bit, the plein-air painter's attitude that the outline of the form was secondary to its internal development, totally changed the character of his procedure and sensibility. Blended with his desire for an immensely powerful and simple monumentality, Cézanne arrived at a new concept of form which used color in a hitherto undreamed-of way. Pissarro had convinced Cézanne to use, as he did, a palette composed only of the three primary colors and their mixtures. Cézanne, however, did not use these hues only to arrive at chromatic equivalents of the lights, middle tones and darks which explain form, but instead for independent planar investigations of the forms in space presented to him by his motif. He used little planes of color traveling over forms and spaces in independent paths to describe the volumes and spaces observed. The independence from one another of their pictorial paths led to distortions of the outlines of forms. These were constantly reworked by the same procedure in a search for simplicity and monumentality. This procedure was responsible for the new plasticity in the developed Cézanne, a plasticity new not only to Cézanne, but, in this form, to the history of art.

Monet, from the 1880s on, did not seek means for expressing form but greater and greater truth to his experience of individual moments of harmony in nature. His haystacks,

Constable: *Study of Sky and Trees*, 1821, oil on paper, 9½ inches high. Victoria & Albert Museum, London.

Constable: *The Hay Wain*, 1821, 57¼ inches high. National Gallery, London.

The Hay Wain, exhibited in Paris at the Salon of 1824, had lasting repercussions on French avant-garde painting, particularly in the case of Delacroix. It was, however, but a pale reflection of his sketches done directly from nature, which Constable did not exhibit.

Courbet: *Forest Pool*, 1860, 60 inches high. Boston Museum. Courbet's use of broad strokes to build volumes influenced the Impressionists.

Boudin: *Dunquerque*, 1889, 14½ inches high.
Clark Art Institute, Williamstown, Mass.

Sisley: *Landscape: Snow Effect*, 1891, 23⅜ inches
high. Clark Art Institute, Williamstown, Mass.

The continuing tradition of plein air and the undoctrinaire
intensification of the landscape experience continue into
the mid-20th century and are still a vital approach today.

the views of Rouen Cathedral and his series based on trees
along the banks of the river Epte all came after this time.
In all of these, each motif remains compositionally the same
or very similar to early compositions from the motif, while
the color, corresponding to changes in light, time of day
and season of the year, changed radically. It is during this
period that Monet's Divisionism begins, influenced by Chevreul's theories of optical mixture. His decision to be influenced by a scientific color theory seems to me not a particularly portentous one. Monet said in England that 90 per
cent of Impressionist theory was already present in the
writings of Ruskin, and prior to Divisionism the Impressionists were already using only the primary hues and colors
derived from mixing them (according to Cézanne, through
the influence of Pissarro). Monet chose Chevreul because
his theory was a useful tool in the path he had already taken,
the production of paintings emphasizing as intensely as
possible the experience of light and air at a given moment.

Monet's paintings, particularly from this time forward, are
a peculiarly lyrical and unthreatening version of the Sublime.
The Rouen Cathedrals and the trees by the Epte series seem
to have vertical extensions; the haystacks and Thames series,
horizontal ones—although some of the Thames paintings
seem to continue on all four edges, as do many of the
Nymphéas. All of these paintings were produced with an
impasto and a visible brushstroke which never lets the
observer forget that they are painted. Although forms become indistinct and blend together, that into which they
blend is most typically a glowing, jewel-like whole. The
identification of the shapes which make up the composition
with the surface of the canvas, the obvious stroke of the
brush and the colors, unlike any ordinarily perceived by the
viewer in nature, all combine to give the painting the char-

acter of an object, and not an illusionistic representation of
an observed scene. The seeming expansion of the canvas
could thus be perceived without threat and with elation.
His verticality and horizontality of the composition, together
with the function of the brushstroke and of color, has been
more influential on 20th-century abstraction than on figurative painting. Consciously or not, Monet's influence is felt
in the works of Rothko, Newman, Noland, the late Hofmann,
and the Guston of the early 1950s.

Alfred Sisley apparently never painted a large picture. He
never accepted Divisionism nor developed as eccentric a
style as did Cézanne. He continued the tradition of Corot
and the Barbizon school and more particularly that of Boudin and Jongkind. In his attempt to extract the essential
qualities of the scene before him, his execution was summary and direct. His simplifications might be radical and
almost coarse, especially in his latest works. He took each
form on its own terms, or rather in terms of the pictorial
tradition which came to him from Barbizon. He tried to
catch the character of light at a given time and place with
the specific atmospheric quality of the moment. He could
not distort the forms as Cézanne did, nor exaggerate the
color as in Monet, but instead sought for the simplest and
most direct expression of the scene.

Monet's influence after the Fauves was not felt again
until the Abstract-Expressionists. Cézanne had a profound
influence on the course of 20th-century painting, through
the Cubists and other abstract painters. It is true that he did
influence Vlaminck and Derain in his brushstroke landscape
paintings; but they, together with Soutine in his later work,
Vuillard particularly in his later work and Albert Marquet,
blend a respect for the particulars of nature with an intensity
of emotion and a directness of expression which, like that

Marquet: *Pont St. Michel*, 1920, 28¾
inches high. Private collection, France.

Constable: *View on the Stour: Dedham Church in the Distance*, ca. 1830-36,
pencil and sepia wash, 8 inches high. Victoria & Albert Museum, London.

Monet: *Rouen Cathedral, West Façade*, 1894, 39½ inches high.
National Gallery, Washington, D.C. Chester Dale Collection.

It is amazing to find at the very beginning of plein-air painting a drawing by Constable as charged with light
as those Matisse was to achieve in the 20th century. Monet's painting, today considered typically Impressionist
but actually done after the Impressionist group began to break up, is one of his most radical color statements.

An early and startlingly modern example of plein-air painting: Constable's *Study of Tree Trunks,* ca. 1821, oil on paper, 9¾ inches high. Victoria & Albert Museum, London.

The Outer Light

of Sisley, seeks above all to remain true to the experience of the subject before them.

Plein-air painting as a rigid doctrine is now a part of history. Besides providing traditions which help determine the procedure and character of 20th-century landscape painting, plein-air or not, the 19th-century landscapists opened the way for radical 20th-century abstract art. To choose but two examples, Kandinsky and Mondrian, the

character of the compositions of both, the use of color in Kandinsky, and the development of passages in Mondrian, point back to the years preceding both artists' first major abstract work when both were landscape painters, sketched and painted out-of-doors, working within the plein-air modes of the 19th century. Abstract painting in both color and composition flows naturally and directly from the landscape painting of the 19th century.

Plein-air portraits of a plein-air painter: Sargent's *Monet Painting in His Studio-Boat,* ca. 1889 (private collection). **Left:** Manet's version of the same subject, 32 inches high. Neue Pinakothek, Munich.

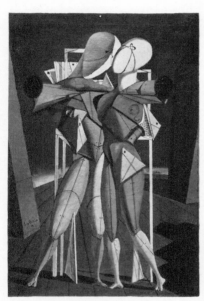

De Chirico's *Hector and Andromache,* 1917, 35½ inches high: light from different sources falling on the figures, contrasting to a greenish twilight on the horizon, evokes a "metaphysical" atmosphere. Collection Mattioli Foundation, Milan.

Magritte's *Domain of Lights, 2,* 1950, 31 inches high: light as a subject for invented improbability. Museum of Modern Art, New York.

In Tanguy's *Mama, Papa Is Wounded!,* 1927, 36¼ inches high, the ground plane is defined by a glowing horizon-line, yet the hard shadows cast on the surface indicate a strong light source high over the artist's left shoulder. Museum of Modern Art, New York.

By Nicolas Calas and Elena Calas

In the Light of Dreams

The question "How does the eye see light?" has received various answers. According to Plotinus the eye is a microcosmic sun. This concept inspired John the Evangelist to identify the Logos with Light. Hence, the medieval artist depicted the Divine Word in the form of a ray of light traveling toward the recipient of the Logos—the Virgin of the Annunciation or Saul, blinded by a luminous ray, falling off his horse. Painting had to wait for Caravaggio's *Conversion of St. Paul* to be depicted with a poignancy worthy of the perturbations experienced by a great visionary. Unlike the Gothic ray of light that symbolizes Truth, Caravaggio's chiaroscuro encompasses an extraordinary event in a dramatic structure. Caravaggio filled the need of an age that apprehended truth in terms of history. When scientific truth took precedence over both the theological and the historical, it was discovered by Thomas Young that the cones of the eye respond to three primary colors, red, green and blue, while yellow is produced by the effective mixing of red and green. Since these results were obtained by mixing lights, they were of no use to the painter who mixes pigments and who obtains green by combining blue and yellow. All such physical theories of colors were rejected by Goethe. Echoing Plotinus he asked, "How could we see light if the eye were not sunlike?" For Goethe, Truth is a revelation emerging at the point where the inner world of man meets eternal reality. The doctrine that the eye is a microcosmic sun is based on the belief, shared by Plotinus and Goethe, that God is not only outside us but also within us. Stripped of its metaphysical context, Goethe's theory of colors is based on the antithesis between light and darkness, i.e. yellow and blue, the former emerging when light yields to darkness and the latter when darkness yields to light.

Since Nietzsche, identifying himself with a prophet of fire and light, announced that God was dead, inner light could no longer be identified with truth. In his famous Cubist manifesto, Apollinaire compared painting to fire for, like the flame, painting possesses the incontestable truth of its own light. He draws the conclusion that Cubism is metaphysical painting, meaning by this that it is a conceptual art, not a sensuous imitation of reality. No wonder that he could proclaim in somewhat Nietzschean terms that the artists are, "above all, men who want to become inhuman." It is in the light of Apollinaire's manifesto that we best understand what de Chirico and his group really meant when they spoke of their anti-Futurist painting as being Metaphysical.

Apollinaire not only reinterpreted the term metaphysical but also invented the term Surrealism; he is a spiritual father of both Giorgio de Chirico and of André Breton. Unlike the term Metaphysical, Surrealism is free from theological connotations. Breton adopted the new word to express a synthesis between two conflicting realities, the dream's reality and physical reality. On the strength of Freud's *Interpretation of Dreams*, Breton assigned to conceptual art the role of creating shock effects. Breton agreed with Apollinaire that de Chirico was the first to sense that in our time inevitability comes as a shock. It is through de Chirico that most artists who did not stem from Dadaism came to Surrealism.

De Chirico

De Chirico viewed the world through the eyes of Nietzsche, who maintained that the death of God was an event that "cast a great shadow over Europe." An artist of de Chirico's generation could feel that his mission was "to wander back, treading in the footsteps by which humanity made its great suffering journey through the desert past" in order to learn "where it is that future humanity cannot tread and should not tread again" (*The Wanderer and his Shadow*). Being an unbeliever, de Chirico could not trace this journey back, as did Masaccio, to the *Expulsion of Adam and Eve*. In his re-

Nicolas Calas, born in Greece, was one of the youngest members of the original Surrealist group in Paris in the 1930s, and emigrated with them to New York at the beginning of World War II. Poet, polemicist, historian, he has published two books of essays and is Associate Professor of Art History at Fairleigh Dickinson College, Rutherford, N.J. His wife, **Elena Calas,** collaborated with him on a book on Peggy Guggenheim's art collection, and is writing a series of articles on Bosch.

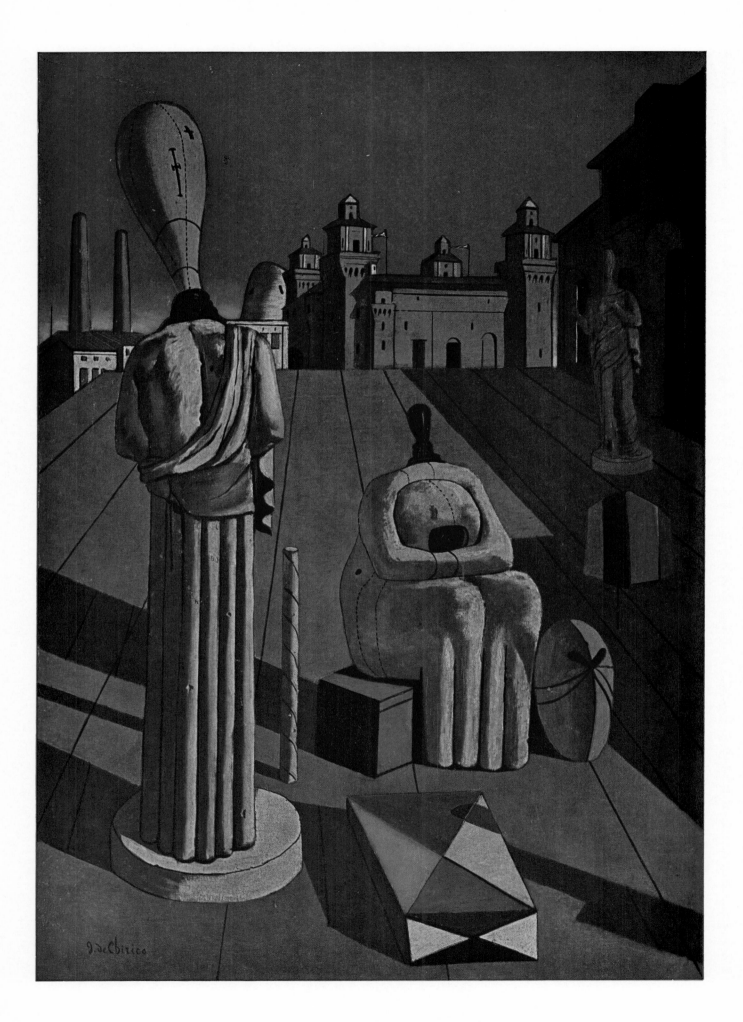

interpretation of this famous painting de Chirico presents us with faceless mannequins in such works as *Duo* and *Hector and Andromache*. Why this re-creation? Nietzsche supplies an answer: "Name it: Whatever I have to offer to you—'Re-creation? re-creation?'—'You are inquisitive! What are you saying!' 'But give, please.'—'What? What? Say it! Another mask! a second mask!'" *(Beyond Good and Evil)*. Are de Chirico's mannequins of cylinders, spheres and triangles a warning that we should not tread on the false path of Cubism?

Wandering back, de Chirico carefully scrutinized quattrocento paintings of sharply delineated shadowless streets, squares and houses. In *Hector and Andromache*, the face of each figure is lit up by a different source of light, one from the front and the other from the right. The shadows cast from the buildings and those by the mannequins are at variance. The light falling on the figures, contrasting to

the greenish crepuscular light on the horizon, envelops the picture in a "metaphysical" atmosphere.

Similar contrasts in the direction of shadows and light at the close of the day are exploited in *The Disquieting Muses*. How disturbing to see the shadow of the building abruptly end before the sunlit castle and to realize that the castle and the factory on the left stand on a ground below the level of the square. This is a mystifying device de Chirico resorted to frequently. In his famous *Pink Tower*, he subtly combines two viewpoints, that of an observer in the middle of the court, and that of one looking at a distant landscape from within a second-floor room. That de Chirico could have resorted to the ingenious practice of combining two viewpoints is suggested by his statement: "A landscape closed within the arch of a portico or within the frame of the rectangle of the window assumes a vast metaphysical value since it is solidified and set apart from the surround-

Giorgio de Chirico: *The Disquieting Muses*, 1917, 38¼ inches high. Collection Mattioli Foundation, Milan.

In de Chirico's *Pink Tower*, 1913, 29½ inches high, the equestrian statue is a black silhouette while its pedestal reflects the sun. Peggy Guggenheim Collection, Venice.

ing space" (Giorgio de Chirico, "Il senso architectonico nella pittura antica").

Magritte

Magritte's "visible poetry" embraces many depictions of the sky, sometimes somber, even menacing, very occasionally misty, most often a deep summer blue with floating cumulus clouds. Landscape or interior or an enigmatic combination of the two (as in *Personal Values*, 1952), however brightly lit and carefully shadowed, seldom displays the source of light. In his famous series on the *Domain of Lights,* Magritte treats light in much the same manner as he treats other improbabilities which he invents for our mystification: the artist brings together mutually exclusive opposites—a sunlit noonday sky with scattered white clouds and the landscape below plunged in darkness, but for lit windows in barely visible façades and a street-lamp casting a small glow.

Among the great paintings of the "Granite" period, some yield a side-light, literally, on Magritte's variations on the subject. In the foreground of a vast plain in *Memory of a Voyage,* 1955, a monument-like candlestick is surrounded by a loose circle of boulders. The candlestick is of granite with a granite candle and a flame of granite which gives no light. The plain merges dimly with a sky heavily overcast on the horizon. If we are to judge by the short shadows cast by candlestick and boulders, it is nearly noon. In *Memory of a Voyage, 3,* 1951, the granite interior of a room, highly illuminated by an invisible source of light from the left, centers on a still-life consisting of a granite table with granite tablecloth, fruit, book, bottle and glass, casting strong shadows, as does the vertical boulder conglomeration seen through an open window—a precipitous canyon whose source of light is altogether inexplicable. In another *Memory of a Voyage,* 1955, the still-life is relegated to the background, with a granite frocked gentleman (Marcel Lecomte) and a granite lion occupying the center stage. The still-life on the table has been reduced to the vase of fruit and a candle in a candlestick. This time it is the stone flame from the stone candle which throws full light on the table-top, raises quasi-appropriate shadows from the candlestick and vase and illuminates the framed picture of a canyon hanging above the table. However, it may be questioned whether it is *the* source of light: witness the clarity with which the lion's pensive face is presented to the viewer.

Delvaux

Impelled by his reaction to Magritte's work, Paul Delvaux staked out his dreamland inhabited by somnambulistic, wide-eyed, self-engrossed, "great immobile women," as they were celebrated by Eluard in a poem dedicated to Delvaux. From de Chirico, Delvaux adapted to his needs the Italianate urban vistas and the effects of light and shadow. With Delvaux, bright sunlight is the exception; his is the pale light of a dark day or the cold moonlight of a clear night. Shadows cast by the women, by trees and posts, are hauntingly repetitive—just as the women themselves are multiples of the

In René Magritte's *Personal Values,* 1952, 31⅝ inches high, the wardrobe mirror reveals the light source, an infrequent occurrence in his pictures of interiors, however brightly lit and carefully shadowed. Collection Harry Torczyner, New York.

Magritte's *Memory of a Voyage,* 1955, 63⅞ inches high, is one of several pictures having a stone candle with a stone flame, which here, unusually, is the source of light. Museum of Modern Art, New York.

In *Night Train*, 1947, 60 inches high, Paul Delvaux has both an elaborate chandelier and the conical light of a shaded lamp. Collection Mr. and Mrs. Allen Guiberson, Dallas, Tex.

In Delvaux's *Nocturne*, 1939, 37 inches high, a strong frontal light bathes the women, contradicting the background shadows. Collection Peter A. De Maerel, New York.

One. He delights in Dali as a miniaturist. Delvaux himself is obsessively intent on an exact and elaborate depiction of objects, whether it be trains and tramways, gas-lit interiors, brocades and laces, skeletons or Greek temples. With the same singular precision he depicts light sources: candles, kerosene lamps, chandeliers, street lights, light-shedding windows and doorways. Yet, in landscapes such as *The Echo*, 1943, the crescent moon can scarcely account for the strong illumination of the vistas of columned buildings, the precisely delineated balustrade and paved road, and in no way explains the bright light bathing the luminous bodies of the women advancing towards the spectator. In the case of a painter as dedicated to precision as Delvaux, a good elucidation of the dilemma of a double source of light has been offered by the critic René Gaffé: "Even in his earliest, darkest works which are sometimes lit only by a flame of a lamp, light is present without our being able to guess at its source . . . For there is light and light. Thus a canvas can be luminous without being immersed in brightness. One of the constant preoccupations of Delvaux is his search for this effect."

Dali

In *The Secret Life of Salvador Dali*, Dali describes experiments that as a student he made with effects of light. He discovered that he could produce dazzling whites by scratching with a penknife an area previously daubed with a brush soaked in India ink and that luminous effects of colors are produced best by impastos of the color itself, deliberately piled on canvas.

Dali's contrasts between figures and their shadows are famous: the latter are made to look at least as solid as the object that cast them. Some of Dali's most striking effects result from a combination of two sources of light, the one obviously coming from a natural, albeit invisible, source and the other from an arbitrary one intended to be confused with the natural one. His *Woman Sleeping in a Landscape* is obviously inspired by Man Ray's well-known photograph, *Primacy of Matter over Mind*. While Man Ray's photograph suggests dematerialization of the forms of a woman who seems to be melting and spreading, Dali's suggests despiritualization through materialization. While de Chirico's main objective was to create a sense of mystery, Dali is intent on shattering illusions. This is not the dreamlike vision of a lovely naked girl asleep on a coastal plain. Her nudity is no longer protected by the darkness of night, and the light that is falling upon her is a photographer's spotlight. It should be recalled that Dali often said that he wanted to produce "handmade photographs."

In *Sleep*, 1938, Dali uses two sources of light as is indicated by the conflicting directions followed by the shadows. While the shadows in the foreground are slanted forward from left to right, those in the brighter middle ground slant backward, also from left to right. The giant crutch against the sky, at extreme right, reflects a metallic glow while the castle below stands shadowless. By means of antitheses, the soft giant sleeping figure acquires the appearance of a huge curtain falling over the stage of daylight.

Ernst

Sun or moon over forest and sea recur persistently during the years that Max Ernst resorted to the frottage technique, whose possibilities he discovered in 1925. Most effectively, perhaps, the moon is paired with a forest. Ernst conjures up his unnatural forests and endows them with celestial disks which may or may not account for light penetrating the petrified depths to afford us a glimpse of their denizens or for the glitter of surfaces; exceptionally, there is no hint of a source of illumination for the hard reflections of *Bird In the Heart of the Forest* and *Tibulary Forest*, both 1928. Con-

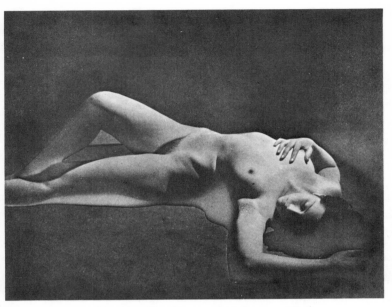

Man Ray: *The Primacy of Matter over Mind,*
1931, solarized photograph.

Salvador Dali: *Woman Sleeping in a Landscape,* 1931,
10⅝ inches high. Peggy Guggenheim
Foundation; Solomon R. Guggenheim Museum, New York.

Max Ernst: *Europe After the Rain,* 1940-42, 21½ inches high: a vegetable-mineral
phantasmagoria brightly lit by an unseen sun. Wadsworth Atheneum, Hartford, Conn.

Dali: *Sleep,* 1937, 20 inches high: a huge curtain falling over the stage of daylight. Collection Edward H. James, Los Angeles.

versely, in *Bright Night,* 1927, the moon appears sufficiently high to account for the luminosity.

In his earlier Forests, Ernst delights in the extra mystification provided by his moons and suns. In *Forest, Bird, Sun,* ca. 1926, a ringed disk is slipped around one "tree"—a carbonized plank—like a ring on a finger; it ostensibly throws light on a dotted outline of a bird with a disk for an oversize eye. In *Forest,* 1926, an elaborate moon is in front of a dark mass of trees: it is not just ringed but twice encircled and through the outer circle, a transparent one, some of the forest is dimly perceived. Ernst's titles usually make clear whether the disk is meant to be that of sun or moon, but he also is apt to make visual distinctions: the dark core of a moon is encircled by a large white ring in *The Great Forest,* 1927, while the tones are reversed for a sun, as in *The Sea and the Sun* of 1926-1927.

As a Dadaist, Ernst had made collages titled *Dada Sun, Dada Forest,* using a blue knob and an intricate wheel as replacements for the sun. His adaptation of decalcomania

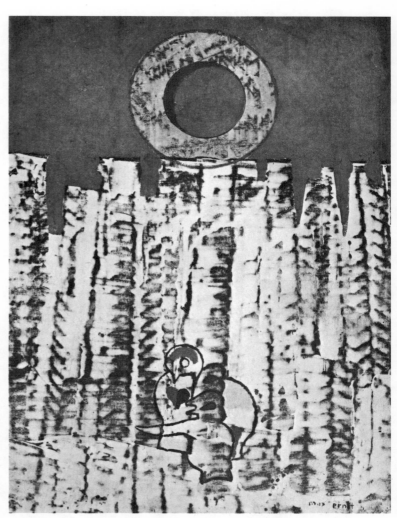

Ernst: *The Great Forest,* 1927, 45 inches high. Kunstmuseum, Basel.

In Ernst's *Bird in the Heart of the Forest,* 1928, the dark celestial disk can hardly be the light source for the hard reflections. Collection Robert Lebel, Paris.

79

to oil painting in the late '30s opened a new scope of vastness, a phantasmagoria of form and texture, a depth of luminosity, with or without the benefit of a light source. In his famous *Europe after the Rain, 2,* 1940-42, the vegetable-mineral world, illuminated brightly by an unseen sun, rises against a blue sky whose depth is suggested by the layers of floating clouds. In *Rhenish Night,* 1944, a low moon is almost tangled in the extraordinary vegetation; green-tinged light with reflections of orange, blue and purple is just sufficient to pick out in the depth a universe of creatures or rather their gleaming eyes and malevolent profiles. In both his largest canvases and in his tiny "Microbes," Ernst creates gem-like incandescencies in the gorges of unfathomable domains.

Tanguy

Tanguy was overwhelmed by his first sight of a de Chirico in 1923; in his own work he first cast shadows some three years later. He continued to evoke a determinedly menacing semi-darkness in paintings titled appropriately *Storm, or, Black Landscape,* 1926, *Extinction of Useless Lights,* 1927, *The Dark Garden,* 1928, *The Lurid Sky,* 1928. (Most of the

Yves Tanguy: *Imaginary Numbers,* 1954, 39⅛ inches high. Pierre Matisse Gallery, New York.

titles of the works of this period remain unknown, while some later ones were suggested by André Breton.) In what appears to be a largely submarine domain, the spotlights and glows are of undetermined origin; restless protozoan creatures co-exist with more static and solid, shadow-casting objects. In his famed *Mama, Papa is Wounded!,* 1927, primordial ooze—temporarily at least—has solidified into a hard surface manifestly able to support the hard black shadows, a plane defined by a glowing horizon-like line. But what about the bone-like object above that line?

Having divided submarine densities from *terra firma* and fleetingly emerged into full sunlight in his versions of the North African landscape, Tanguy went on to merge earth and sky in those enchanted horizonless vistas, mostly in pearl-grey, shot with pale or radiant hues, sparsely populated by intricate artifacts of delightful color combinations. The low-toned backgrounds and the fragile objects do not accord with the heavy shadows: those must be understood as projecting the mystery of distances. Upon his coming to live in the United States, Tanguy's palette underwent a considerable change: Tanguy himself attributed the intensification of color to the strong light here. In those works, the invisible source of light, always back of the artist, quite consistently projects shadows to the left, while in the earlier paintings light emanated from behind either his right or his left shoulder.

Subsequently, Tanguy's constructions, greatly enlarged, took possession of the foreground, at first in a silvery, benign light, then progressively so dark and cluttered as to eliminate the effectiveness or possibility even of shadows. In a painting shortly preceding his death, *Multiplication of the Arcs,* 1954, the tight cemetery-like conglomeration of stones is suffocatingly oppressive despite patches of near-pastel hues; long stark white slabs largely replace shadows and the black horizon sharply divides earth from sky—seemingly forever.

Miro

While de Chirico casts dramatic shadows upon a forum, Miro, with a healthy Fauve appetite for color, enlivens playfully or savagely fanciful silhouettes.

Against a yellow sky, as intense as the bluest can be, *Mrs. Mills in 1750,* dressed in dark green and brown, dances before our eyes as a vision of lightness and gaiety. In contrast, *Seated Woman,* 1932, depicts a multicolored silhouette against a black wall, bright under a small window with a blue crescent moon. When Miro's silhouettes become transparent, as in *Woman, Bird, Stars,* 1942, they glow, as does the background. Light is both hazy and intense, brightening a night shrunk to a few patches of black and scrawls of stars. In *Still-life with Old Shoe,* 1937, (Miro's *Guernica* according to Jacques Dupin), the artist exceptionally resorts to an apocalyptic light. A battle of yellow and green illuminates the *nature-morte:* an old shoe, a heel of bread, a bottle of

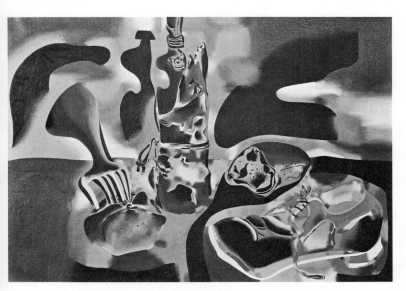

Joan Miró: *Still-life with Old Shoe*, 1937,
32 inches high. Collection James Thrall Soby.

Miró's *Portrait of Mrs. Mills in 1750* (after the prototype
by a pupil of Reynolds), 1929, 45½ inches high. Private coll.

wine, a fork avidly biting into a potato, all casting ominously
thick black shadows.

Masson

André Masson has said that "light is the skin of painting, the
quivering epiderm secretly related to our substance." While
living in America during World War II, Masson made what
are probably his best Surrealist paintings. Meditating on the
design of Indian blankets, he loosened contours to fit his
mood of a somber Fauve. The absence of empty space in
his cluttered world of forms and superimposed images is
compensated by the intensity of areas in primary colors, a
brightness obtained by thickening the coat of paint or adding tiny grains of glass.

Duchamp and Matta

With *The Bride Stripped Bare by Her Bachelors, Even,* Marcel
Duchamp turned Impressionism inside out and Cubism up-
side down. What is the relation between the transparent and
opaque sections of the *Glass?* How is the inscribed portion
of the *Glass* to be correlated to what is seen through the
glass? Duchamp's transparent title becomes opaque when
we try to explain the picture in terms of Bachelors disrobing

a Bride. Duchamp was implying that the role of the artist is
to perplex, not to solve problems. To a translucency
achieved through dissolution of colors or volumes, Duchamp
opposes a confusing transparency.

Matta was the first artist to understand the implications
of this work. In a study of *The Bride Stripped Bare by Her
Bachelors, Even,* (written in collaboration with Katherine
Dreier), Matta explains that it is a work in which painting,
glass and mirror "are the three substances in dynamic inter-
relation to the final image of the glass . . . While we gaze
upon the Bride there appears through the glass the image
of the room wherein we stand and in the radiation of the
mirror design lives the image of our own body."

In his painting, *The Bachelors Twenty Years After,* 1943,
Matta created what he called four-dimensional space. He
was primarily interested in doing for space what the Cubists
had done for volume. In *Vertigo of Eros,* 1944, the picture
becomes a structure of transparent planes. In contradistinc-
tion to Braque, who in his Analytical Cubist period adapts Neo-
Impressionist techniques to produce effects of transition
from light to shadow, Matta colors his transparent planes to
bewilder the viewer with ambiguous effects of multidimen-
sional space.

In such paintings as *The Revolt of Opposites,* Matta used
light and dark angular planes as if anchored to a transparent

Duchamp: *The Bride Stripped Bare by Her Bachelors Even (The Large Glass)*; 1915-23, replica 1966; 107 inches high.

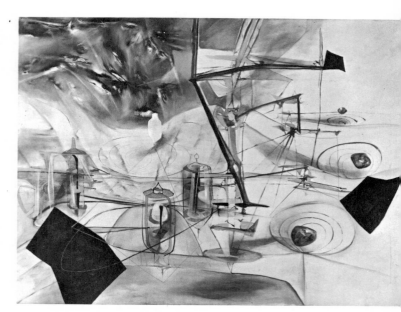

In *The Bachelors Twenty Years After,* 1943, 37 15/16 inches high, Matta carried his understanding of Duchamp into the creation of what he called four-dimensional space. Coll. Mr. and Mrs. George H. Hamilton, Williamstown, Mass.

surface through which we see a whirling world with elements borrowed from Duchamp's *Glass*.

Matta's speculations on problems posed by Duchamp led him to develop an elaborate and difficult pictorial composition. It was this purely formal aspect of his work, to the exclusion of all considerations of illusionistic effects of light and transparency, that influenced Arshile Gorky. What else are the two versions of Gorky's *Betrothal* but a reinterpretation of the Duchamp-Matta problem in "formal" terms?

Klapheck

Konrad Klapheck lives in a world in which sewing machines, typewriters, telephones, drills and adding machines impose their will upon mankind. Anchored to the bottom of the canvas, a sewing machine is apt to lift its monumental form to the sky or to thrust back an indefinable background. *War,* 1965, *Soldiers' Brides,* 1967, and *Female Tyrant,* 1967, confront the viewer with glowing pride; never betraying the slightest trace of shadow or doubt. A reflected light is the only possible source of illumination. Klapheck has dramatized the brightness of light falling upon the machine's cylindrical forms by abolishing all distinction between the highlights and the shadows, either to pass abruptly from bright-

ness to darkness, as in *Soldiers' Brides,* or indirectly by means of an even grey, as in *War*. Klapheck has given a fearsome superego to a machine that the Dadaists had eroticized, and he has metamorphosed the optimistic world of Léger into a cruelly Surreal one.

Illuminations

In Surrealist terms, Plotinus' remark that the eye is a microcosmic sun could be reinterpreted to mean that through this ocular sun, dreams of the night and visions of the day are illuminated. This is the meaning that should be attributed to Eluard's beautiful line, *"dormir, la lune dans un oeil et le soleil dans l'autre."*

To evoke his dreams and· to provoke a corresponding response from a viewer of his painting, the artist must resort to subterfuges to convey that which is never seen by normal physical light but only in sleep or in a state of ecstasy (i.e., out of place). The painter must suggest that the depicted is both too improbable to be comprehended as real and too impressive to be dismissed as nonsense. Surrealist paintings are "illuminated" by: paradoxical juxtapositions of light and shadow, by multiple sources of light, by translucency, by phosphorescent luminosity.

Konrad Klapheck's *War*, 1965, 57 inches high, is dramatized by abrupt transitions from intense highlights to deep shadows. Janis Gallery, New York.

In *Vertigo of Eros*, 1944, 77 inches high, Matta creates a multi-dimensional swirl of colored transparent planes. Museum of Modern Art, New York.

Arshile Gorky: *Bethrothal, 1,* 1947, 51½ inches high. Collection Mr. and Mrs. Taft Schreiber, Beverly Hills.

In André Masson's *Meditation on an Oak Leaf,* 1942, 40 inches high, density of forms is offset by intense colors brightened by tiny grains of glass. Museum of Modern Art, New York.

Antonio Gaudi (1852-1926), brilliant Catalan, whose extravagant architecture was both radical and eclectic.

The Sagrada Familia (Temple of the Holy Family), Barcelona, a traditional cathedral in its form, permeated by neo-medieval symbolism, is in many ways Gaudi's most conservative work, yet it is strikingly eccentric in appearance. The structure and the realistic statues which adorn it are engulfed by Gaudi's characteristic melting undulation of stone surfaces. Legibility is overwhelmed by intense abstract light patterns. Gaudi intended it to be brightly colored, but died before the work could be finished. This transept façade of the Nativity, the only completed portion, is the murky, rosy brown of native stone. From left to right the portals symbolize Hope, Charity, Faith.

By Robert Descharnes and Clovis Prévost

The Last Cathedral

At the end of the last century, Catalonia and particularly Barcelona experienced an extraordinary movement of spiritual renewal, both economic and political, in the arts and in the crafts. Out of the surge of this Catalan renaissance came the Temple of the Holy Family, the shrine and symbol of the new Barcelona.

The Sagrada Familia rose little by little in a sparsely populated section, between the old quarter of the Port and the hills on the outskirts. Campaigns for donations were organized throughout the city to finance the project. All Barcelona came to visit the construction site as work advanced. The workers of the neighborhood became masons, stonecutters, models for the ornamental sculptures. And despite the economic difficulties which arose, the first façade was completed amid popular fervor like that which accompanied the building of Gothic cathedrals. In devoting more than 43 years of his life to the construction of the Temple of the Sagrada Familia, Antonio Gaudi is doubtless the last of the cathedral builders. A recluse in his temple from 1906 until his death 20 years later, this master-architect remained for a long time little-known and misunderstood. But he was one of the first to have forcefully reaffirmed the pre-eminence of architecture as the art which organizes space and thus governs the quality of all other forms of expression. And he was the first to have successfully imposed his "author's imperialism" down to the last detail, and to think out the relationship between object and environment. He became by turns painter, musician, sculptor, cabinetmaker, iron-worker and city-planner. For him the architect is a "visionary seer" who alone can accomplish "the total work of art." In this sense Gaudi is absolutely not a functionalist, and is opposed in theory to the majority of contemporary architects who design "machines for living." For him, everything in architecture is subjugated to the inventive mind, and only a poetic universe is habitable. Gaudi opened the door to let in dreams.

In 1900, the poet Joan Maragall wrote:
The Temple seems to rise all by itself as a tree is born in slow majesty . . . The Portal of the burgeoning temple is marvelous; not architecture but pure poetry. It seems not to be a construction of man but the earth itself, the stone trying to lose its inertia, and already beginning to have meaning, confusedly to produce images, representations of earth and sky, amid a sort of murmur of stone . . .

Ornamentation

"Treat building naturalistically, that is, conceive of it so that it is the expression of the forces that are at work inside it," wrote Gaudi. Proceeding precisely in this way, he bent traditional materials (stone, brick, ceramic) to the demands of a personal style. The elements of construction are assimilated to a decorative system and are part of an organic whole. He himself said that "organizing space is not merely building structures, but covering them, making them live and above all making them lose their materiality, spiritualizing them through a living ornamentation." Gaudi's enthusiam for the naturalism of forms is limitless. For him there is no other transcendence than that contained in the substance itself, on his native Catalan soil.

Polychromy

From the earliest times polychromy has been an essential element of Catalonian architecture. Gaudi replanted this tradition in Mediterranean culture and intended his Temple to be embellished with color. Greek monuments were painted, and we know that their colors were made still brighter by the use of beeswax. Gaudi declared the Sagrada Familia issued from the purest tradition of Hellenic art, and he sought to give it esthetic properties: clarity and rhythm of line, harmony of proportion, vigor of forms emphasized by color.

The brightest colors were to be reserved for the lower parts of the Temple, those least accessible to the sun. The

Robert Descharnes is a Paris photographer known for his photographs of contemporary art and artists.
He has made films on the work of Dali and Mathieu, and is the author of books on Dali and Rodin.
Together with his colleague **Clovis Prévost** he has written a book on Gaudi, to be published in Europe by Edita, Lausanne, and in America by Viking.

Gaudi directed Lorenzo Matamala, chief sculptor for the figures and ornamentation, to obtain skeletons, which were then photographed in various positions to study the movement of the human body.

The Last Cathedral

'façade of the Nativity is pierced by three portals. The central porch represents the deep Grotto of Bethlehem, festooned with flowers and fluttering birds. Nebulous shapes emerge from the archivolt which was to be an intense azure, like the sky of a clear winter night, and studded with white almond blossoms and sparkling stars. The constellations of the Zodiac appear in the exact position (Taurus and Gemini) where they were on the night of Christ's birth, with the great carved star of the East above the *pesebre,* or Catalan crèche.

The central archivolt of the façade was to be painted a deep blue like the pediments of Greek temples, so that the shadows of the statues would disappear and their brilliant colors stand out. The architectural role of the colors was to be subordinate to symbolic and liturgical meaning.

On the right is the Gate of Hope with the Flight into Egypt; it is also the portal nearest to the sea. It is consecrated to the marine kingdom, with lotus, papyrus, palm trees, ducks and the web-footed sea-turtle. The vegetation

of the Nile was to burst forth in green and purplish-blue tones near the top.

The left-hand portal is the Gate of Faith, with Jesus as a carpenter's apprentice; it opens to the north, toward the hills of Catalonia. Consecrated to the terrestrial kingdom with the flora and fruits of the fields, its brushy vegetation and the tortoise with claw feet, the Gate of Faith was to be sienna colored, like the sands of Palestine.

Inside the Temple, the east aisle was to be covered with white and gold mosaics, symbolizing joy. The west aisle, pierced by the Gate of the Passion, was meant to be in tones of black and blue-violet, colors of mourning and penitence.

Realism of Mysticism

"Gaudi sought," wrote José Rafols, "to project an image of life as it is, as though life and art were one and the same thing." Actually Gaudi's method of working may be compared with Dali's when the latter says, "To photograph God

Metal skeleton attached to a wooden crucifix: preliminary study for positioning of the body. The legs were deliberately elongated to compensate for foreshortening and pose.

Crucifix destined for the oratory of Gaudi's Casa Battlo, executed by Carlos Mani under Gaudi's direction in 1907. Its agonized realism is close to Catalan Romanesque tradition.

is an act of faith of the highest purity, in the most profound spiritual tradition of the Middle Ages . . . It is a question of expressing one's vision by an intensely realistic act. Unamuno said it once and for all: 'Realism is the coherence of mysticism!' "

"We ought to consider the criteria of ornamentation in terms of our era," wrote Gaudi in 1878, "of our society, of the geographical space in which they take shape. This ornamentation should be natural, based on our own reasons for existing. It is not a question of imitating just any style, but of creating a system of lines and curves in harmony with the topographical, climatological and meteorological conditions of the place; it is this which constitutes a style."

The column is the bole, the trunk; the roof is the mountain with its flanks and its dome; the vault is the grotto; the walls of cliffs form lintels and corbels through the erosion of their softer layers.

It is thus that the Sagrada Familia lifts into the sky of Barcelona its palm fronds, its stone wheat, its buds and stalks of poppies picked at the base of the cathedral. A smooth boulder from Montserrat towers over the Gate of Hope. A swarm of birds with outspread wings makes the facade palpitate. Drops of blood and dew trickle down the surface. Birds, branches, stars, buds—as though dipped in paste—seem to emerge from the mass of the edifice.

The architect wrote: "The formal elements of a work should fuse, merge, fit together within the whole: lose their individuality and give it further unity. Continuous forms are perfect forms."

Structure and Form

For Gaudi, sculpture assumed its full significance only when integrated into the body of an edifice. Architecture and sculpture regulated according to the same laws, the same conceptual plan, may then attain organic unity. We see the same process of construction in both. Just as the edifice is first of all a rigorous structure, then an enveloping sculp-

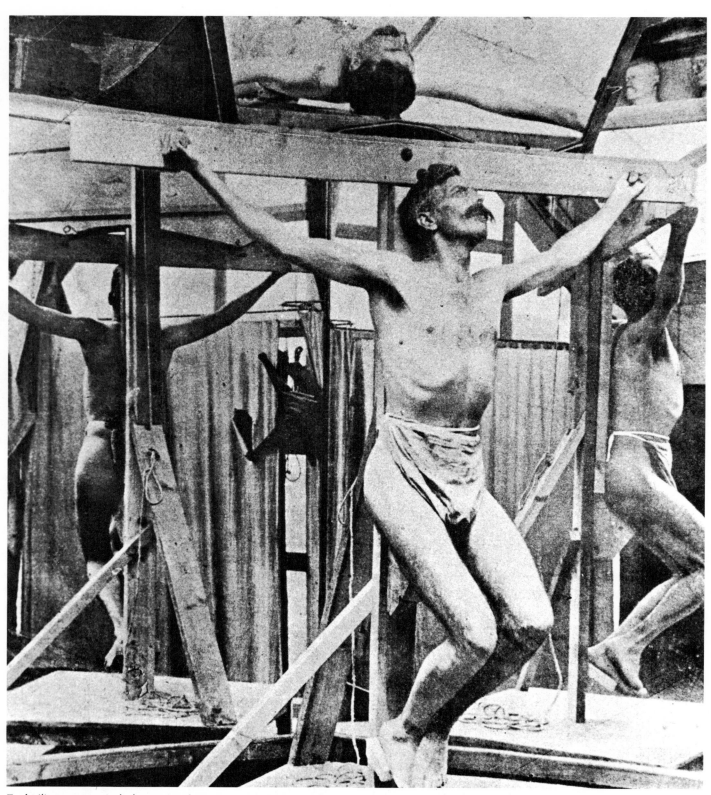

To facilitate anatomical observation from many viewpoints, Gaudi set his models up surrounded by mirrors. The model being studied here was a foreman of the stonecutters working on the Temple; to Gaudi, he embodied Christ, and was the same age.

"The statue is not a moment of action; it will be the entire act condensed": photos like
this one were taken of the mirror studies to aid in the analysis of movement.

ture and finally polychromy, so statuary was for Gaudi first a skeleton, then form, finally color. Every form is the envelope of an interior structure. The latter is fundamental. This is why Gaudi attributed so much importance to the study of the skeleton which structures the human body.

"The expression of the form is given and structured by the skeleton," wrote Gaudi, "for it is the variable element in it. The rest is only details which disappear at a certain distance. The skeleton is a mobile structure; one must consider it under its two aspects through the direct study of the bone-structure and that of man's movement . . . The statue is not a moment of action; it will be the entire act condensed."

Realistic Statuary

Gaudi's intention in building his temple was to address himself to the masses; his statuary with its ultra-clear figuration was destined for the Catalan people. Any man may easily

identify the fauna and flora of his country as sculpted in their simple reality. Gaudi shunned formal abstraction so as to be clear and understood by all. For "the Sagrada Familia was to be the imagery of the Bible, the Book of the Poor."

To seize life in its instantaneity, Gaudi used life-casts and photographs. He obtained the imprint and the outline of reality in its dynamic verity: that is, both as shape and motion. Molds and photographs are methods for analyzing nature: fluttering of wings, smoke, falling forms, the expression of a face. Materials taken from nature itself, animals and people in motion, are studied in their "picturesque reality."

Photographs of his huge stocks of casts, which no longer exist, give an idea of the intensive use Gaudi made of this method. All of them were classified, numbered and stored in the workshops of the Temple and in an adjacent building. They were interchangeable parts and it is possible to mount and assemble them like so many parts of a child's

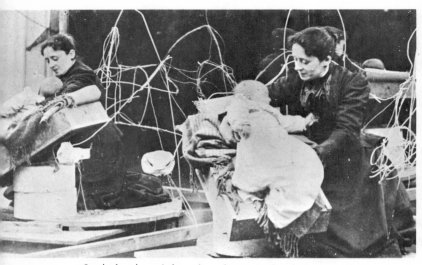 

Study for the crèche: after observing the skeletons, Gaudi sketched the volumes in wire. Here the living models with their wire silhouettes are photographed before hinged mirrors.

Mirror study for an angel musician: seeking prototypes for his figures among the people of the neighborhood, Gaudi used children of a parochial school for his angels.

erector set. Each sculpture represented a Truth, demonstrative and symbolic, in the great academic tradition of the *"pesebres,"* those popular Catalan crèches whose polychrome figures are often casts made from living models. Each figure is seized in an act which from a realistic standpoint is slightly impossible. And what is most surprising is that this sculpture is both an absolutely objective didactic work and a poetic creation. The details are realistic, but the whole attains unreality.

Gaudi sought models for Biblical characters among his neighbors, the people of the *Barri del Poblet,* the workers' quarter of Barcelona. He wished to respect and did come close to traditional Christian iconography. In the countryside around Tarragona, a former Roman colony, he believed he had discovered types of Roman emperors and noblemen, as well as the Greek type in Ampurdan and the Phoenician type among the natives of the island of Ibiza. The workshop of the Temple became a sort of human Noah's ark. The most diverse kinds of people were to be found there, from bishops to ragpickers, bureaucrats and goatherds, waiters, schoolboys and construction workers, painters and poets, even a carter's donkey. Each hoped to become a plaster saint. One of them, a tavern waiter whom Gaudi discovered, posed for the Roman soldier in the Massacre of the Innocents. When this colossus of a man was about to be cast it was discovered that he had six perfect toes on each foot. "I can still see him today," recounts Juan Matamala. "They were going to suppress the extra toes. Gaudi was furious. 'No! No!' he cried. 'He must be cast exactly as he is! It's an anomaly—like slaughtering children!' "

Stages of Sculpture

After preliminary studies on small metal skeletons, Gaudi sketched the volume of the future sculpture with wire. Then a carefully posed model, often accompanied by his wire silhouette, was photographed surrounded by a set of hinged mirrors: this became the sketch for a statue.

The model was then placed in a plaster matrix, but the mold often did not capture the desired movement especially if it was to be expressed by flowing draperies or tresses.

Thus the plaster model was reduced to half-size, and on this maquette cloths were draped; beards and hair, fashioned from hemp coated with plaster, were also attached.

A full-size copy in clay was formed, then molded in plaster so that it could be sawed apart and easily dismantled. The sections were cut at the level of the head, the chest, the waist and the knees, then reassembled, and the whole hoisted into place on the façade.

Following Greek principles, Gaudi corrected the perspective deformations of his statues. Elements which seem to be foreshortened when seen from below were elongated; 5 to 6 centimeters of thickness of stone were added between the sections to obtain, by trial and error, the most harmonious proportions.

After the plaster models were lowered, the corrections were transferred to the rough-hewn blocks of stone, and finally the statue was carved.

Thus the humble parishioners of the Ensanche and the Barri del Poblet were immortalized in the sculpture of the Temple, "as though," writes José Rafols, "life and art were a single entity." Only one spire, consecrated to the apostle Barnaby, was finally finished, a few days before the death of the architect on June 10, 1926.

For several years previously Gaudi had been working with the architects Domingo Sugranes and Francisco Quintina. They took over the direction of the Temple after the master's death. Juan Matamala was appointed to carry out the sculptured groups for the façade. He had learned his craft since childhood in the workshops of the Sagrada

The Last Cathedral

Familia. He continued the sculptures for the Temple until 1935, completing about 20 of the statues planned by Gaudi, and followed his principles to the letter.

The civil war and the death of Sugranes in 1936 brought the work to a halt. The workshops of the Temple were then pillaged and burned. The archives disappeared. All the casts were destroyed; a number of statues on the facade were broken, notably the angel musicians of the central portal. In recent years work has been resumed; the other transept facade is under way; construction continues sporadically.

The Will to Realism

Gaudi's will to realism, his scrupulous exactitude, his respect for nature are above all an act of fervor and humility. What

Next page: Details of the central Portal of Charity containing the crèche. At left, the angels seem to surge from a cliff of living stone, picked out by violent highlights. On the right is the group of the Holy Family, completed long after Gaudi's death, put in place in 1950. The mule and the ornamental motifs around it were cast and sculpted by Lorenzo Matamala under Gaudi's direction; the other figures are later. Above is a massive Star of the East with rays of solidified light hanging below it like stalactites.

Gaudi's studio before its destruction in 1936, showing the reserve of casts, many with interchangeable parts. Some are life-casts, some were made from corpses at a nearby morgue. On the wall are casts of dead babies for the Massacre of the Innocents on the Portal of Hope. Flowers and fruits hanging from the ceiling represent Catalonian flora for the Portal of Faith.

Roman soldier about to impale a child in the Massacre of the Innocents was cast from a neighborhood tavern waiter.

The Last Cathedral

mattered to him were Saints and Angels, "the winged vehicle which leads us to God . . ."

Today the temple of the Sagrada Familia is nothing more than an immense shell. It stands in all its splendor, a grandiose ruin, with its monumental sculptures, its assemblages of geometric shapes and its multitude of symbols.

"I believe," wrote Salvador Dali, "that the Sagrada Familia cannot be finished unless a new genius were to appear . . . To claim that it can be completed in bureaucratic fashion, rationally and without genius, is to betray Gaudi's work. It is far better for it to remain as it is, like a gigantic, decayed tooth, full of possibilities."

Fallen child and head of a goose, another detail of Massacre
of the Innocents, harshly highlighted and densely shadowed by the sun.

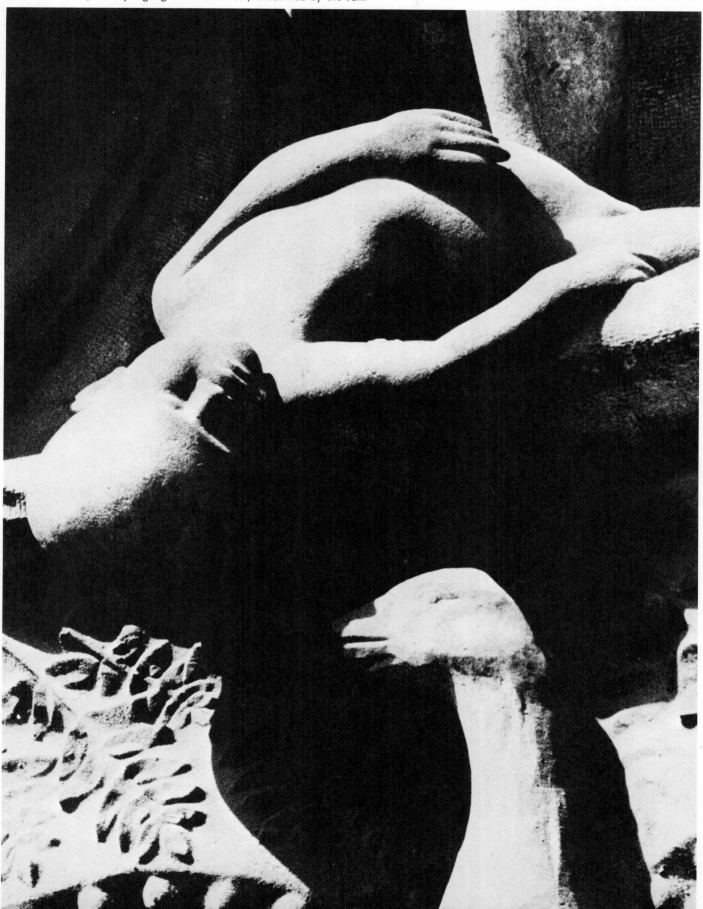

A shaft of light entering a bare room gives an ambience of stark reality to Caravaggio's *The Calling of St. Matthew,* 1598-1601 (128 inches high). San Luigi de' Francesi, Rome.

Georges de La Tour was one of the few Caravaggists to use light in darkness as a source of emotion: *St. Peter Denying Christ,* 1650, 47 inches high, was painted for Marshal La Ferté, Governor of Lorraine. Nantes Museum.

In Gerrit van Honthorst's *The Matchmaker,* 1625 (28 inches high), the impact of Caravaggesque light is softened by the Flemish painter's emphasis on picturesque costume and characterization. Centraal Museum, Utrecht.

By Michael Mahoney

The Discovery of Night

The various ways European painters treated light until the advent of the nineteenth-century plein-air schools already had been evolved or prefigured by the close of the seventeenth century. To refer to that time as the age of the "Baroque" is somewhat confusing. The grandiloquent and theatrical style properly described by the term was only one of several styles that emerged during the century, although it was the most characteristic and one that to varying degrees permeated the styles developing parallel to it. But in addition to the Baroque, the century saw the emergence of Tenebrism, Classicism and—for want of a better word—proto-Romanticism. Light took a varying importance and character in each.

Even at this distance in time, Tenebrism can still be appreciated as having been the century's most strikingly original use of light in relation to what had gone before. Its greatest proponent was Caravaggio, in whose paintings figures are submerged in deep pools of shadow through which a brilliant beam of illumination probes to focus on the central elements of his dramatic compositions. Though to our eyes this may seem a simple device, it does not require great imagination to appreciate how novel and eloquent its effect must have been to his contemporaries. Caravaggio's use of light was utterly different from the sifted, otherworldly light of the Gothic cathedral, from the immutable golden light of the Renaissance ideal, and different from the flickering illumination of Mannerist elegancies and anxieties. The use of darkness in itself was not new—think of the background in Grünewald's *Crucifixion* altarpiece in Colmar (see cover) or Titian's agonized *Crowning with Thorns* in Munich; it was Caravaggio's expressive intent in using darkness that was original. These dark ambients propelled his compositions and therefore his themes into the real, actual world of the observer who, as well, must in many instances have been completely like in appearance to the bearded and gnarled street types the artist deliberately and proudly used

Michael Mahoney was until recently director of publications at the National Gallery, Washington. He now heads the art history department at Trinity College, Hartford, Conn.

for models. When the artist arrived in Rome from Milan about 1590 he worked for a time as a painter of still-lifes and flowers. He must have then cultivated the realism that pervades not only the accoutrements but also the entire conception of such a fully independent work as *Christ at Emmaus.* In seeking to capture the contours, colors and sensations of the penumbrous world at the moment when the risen Christ manifested Himself, Caravaggio eschewed idealization presumably in order that the pious could be reassured thereby that the mysteries of Christ were relatable to the world of air and flesh and light. Some criticized these darkened dramas and use of models drawn from everyday Roman life as banal, indecorous and overly dependent on nature. However Caravaggio's vision was in tune with the Church's post-Trentine aim to bring religion closer to the people and thus, through reform and theological renewal, to recover ground lost to Protestantism. The timeliness of Caravaggio's approach to sacred art and the originality of his style was well recognized by some. He enjoyed a degree of high patronage during his brief career and inspired a generation of painters as far afield as Naples and the Netherlands. However none of these followers equalled him: the master's direct and simple monumentality was too often reduced to the beauteous but merely epicene or enigmatic formulas of a Gentileschi or the overly bombastic statements of a Honthorst. Already in the 1630s Caravaggism was considered an archaizing style in Rome, the city of its origin, though its influence remained strong in provincial centers.

The only seventeenth-century master of comparable stature to use light in any way approaching Caravaggio was Rembrandt. Though Rembrandt never went to Catholic and autocratic Italy and was primarily a painter of Protestant and burgher Holland, the coupling of the two names is not entirely perverse. Like Caravaggio, and similarly in his most mature works, Rembrandt used darkness and focused illumination to concentrate upon the essential expressive elements in his painting, be it upon the tender yet stately reverence in such a religious piece as the *Circumcision,* or upon the elucidation of a sitter's character, both external and internal, as in his magnificent late portraits. Of the many great seicento painters, these two were, to my mind, the most

In the almost total darkness of night, Caravaggio's luridly lit figures heighten the horror of *The Decollation of St. John the Baptist,* 1608, 140¾ inches high. This great late work, still in the place for which it was painted, has recently been cleaned. Cathedral of St. John, La Valetta, Malta.

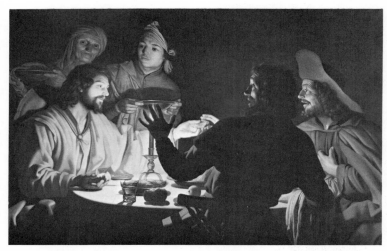

Caravaggesque lighting tends toward the theatrical in *The Supper at Emmaus*, ca. 1630 (47 inches high), variously attributed to either Honthorst or Mathias Stomer. Wadsworth Atheneum, Hartford.

Both the extraordinary treatment of still-life and the rough peasant types relate to the world of reality, in Caravaggio's *Christ at Emmaus*, 1598, 55 inches high (above, detail below). National Gallery, London.

The Discovery of Night

humanizing, the most concerned to make their themes and ideas explicit in naturalistic terms requiring no reference to conceptual or dogmatic authority. In the language of forms available to them, it is interesting to see how each expressed himself similarly through light.

Rembrandt's introspection and Caravaggio's naturalism were both quite out of step with the prevailing style of the century. The idiom of both was very unlike the robust, optimistic, propagandizing, theatrical Baroque style. To the Baroque painters, best exemplified by Rubens in the north or by Pietro da Cortona and Carlo Maratti in the south, light was simply another skein to be interwoven with color, drawing, composition and space to produce their wonderfully movemented set pieces. This was the art of the Church triumphant, the climax of the Catholic Reaction's self-satisfaction at having achieved the goals defined during the Counter Reformation for the revivification of the Church. The theme of Rubens' tapestry sketch celebrates this, for the high priest Melchizedek's presenting Abraham with bread and wine was interpreted as a biblical prefiguration of the ministry of Christ to the world. The style does the same, for as the hegemony of the Church was, in theory, all-pervading and without limits, so this resplendent and sumptuous scene shifts with protean confidence from an architectural setting between columns onto the field of a tapestry unfurled by putti against the architecture. In this kind of painting every element contributes to the over-all effect; no single one predominates over the others.

Light was the sovereign element in Baroque design only in such architectural schemes as Bernini's conception for the apse of St. Peter's. There the light of the Holy Spirit symbolically floods the shrine of Peter's chair—the throne of the popes— through an oculus window depicting the dove of the Paraclete. Bernini frequently exploited light architectonically, either to express a religious concept, as in St. Peter's or in his rendering of the ecstasy of St. Theresa in Santa Maria alla Vittoria; or simply for dramatic purposes, as in his indirect illumination of the side chapels in the richly reveted interior of San Andrea al Quirinale. Later, northern architects, particularly in Catholic Bavaria and Austria, refined this precedent to the point of pyrotechnic virtuosity. They used carefully contrived sources of light to illuminate those ecclesiastical interiors that scintillate like some exquisite porcelain fantasy with gilt, Rococo plaster work and refined pastel coloring. It was only in architecture that light was exploited to such a fruitful and entertaining degree by artists of the Baroque style.

Landscape painters were the century's second group of great artificers in the painting of light. The first of these was Claude Lorrain, a Frenchman resident in Rome. Distantly evocative of Carracci's disciple Domenichino, familiar with the work of Paul Bril and Adam Elsheimer, trained by Agostino Tassi, Claude emerged towards the middle of the seventeenth century as the most monumentalizing and classicizing landscapist of the time. Drawing the landscape of the

Especially in his magnificent late works, Rembrandt uses darkness to focus on the characterization of his sitters: *Margaretha de Geer, Wife of Jacob Trip,* 1661, 51⅜ inches high. National Gallery, London.

Bernini exploited light architectonically in the apse of St. Peter's, Rome, by an oculus window depicting the dove of the Holy Spirit: *Cathedra Petri*, 1657-66, bronze, marble and stucco.

Baroque splendor reaches a climax in Rubens' *The Meeting of Abraham and Melchizedek,* ca. 1625, 26 inches high. National Gallery, Washington, D.C.

Infinite gradations of light convey a classicizing unity of space to Claude Lorrain's
The Judgment of Paris, 1645-46, 44¼ inches high. National Gallery, Washington, D.C.

Roman *campagna* must have sensitized his eye to those extraordinary light effects, at times crisp azure, at others clotted gold, that invest that countryside, depending on the season and time of day. Admiration for Poussin, his compatriot, also living in Rome and the leading classicizing history painter, must have inculcated that love of balanced forms and measured space that is apparent in the way Claude disposed masses of foliage or architecture across and into his picture plane. Purging his compositions of unessential narrative detail, concentrating on august historical or biblical themes, and subordinating all the elements to enhance

those themes, Claude threw over his canvas a scrim of exquisite illumination. Here is a world ennobled, purged of the extraneous and pacified by light. Like the greatest Renaissance luminists of Umbria, Claude used light, the golden light of the ideal, to convey an exalted Olympian dignity.

The landscapes of Salvator Rosa, who also lived in Rome during Claude's lifetime, embody yet another seventeenth-century approach to landscape painting in general and to light in particular: the proto-Romantic. Although his early pictures show compositional borrowings from Claude, Rosa never attempted to imitate the French master's monumen-

In Rembrandt's late work, *The Circumcision of Christ,* 1661, 22½ inches high, bright light shines on the main protagonists of the scene while the accessory figures subside into a shadowy background. National Gallery, Washington, D.C.

Salvator Rosa invented a proto-Romantic landscape quivering with fantasy and ambiguity in staccato accents of light: *Mercury and the Dishonest Woodsman,* ca. 1656, 49½ inches high. National Gallery, London.

Salvator Rosa's fondness for clandestine subjects like his *Night Scene with Figures,* ca. 1660,
20½ inches high, gave him the reputation of consorting with bandits. Wadsworth Atheneum, Hartford.

With dramatic lighting on a live model in suspended motion, the elements of Caravaggio's style are brilliantly assimilated in Orazio Gentileschi's *Young Woman with a Violin*, ca. 1611, 32⅞ inches high. The sitter has been identified as Gentileschi's artist-daughter Artemisia, posing as St. Cecilia. Detroit Institute of Arts.

Vermeer's realization of the diffusion of color in light anticipates Impressionism by two centuries: *Woman in Blue Reading a Letter*, ca. 1665, 18¼ inches high. Rijksmuseum, Amsterdam.

tality. Instead, this truculent artist wrought from his own imagination and in the studio—thus explaining why his landscape drawings are so rare—scenes of umbrageous forests, riven by rock and storm. With confident improvisation Rosa dashed across his canvases richly textured colors and light pregnant with moodiness and ambiguity. In his sometimes murky, sometimes golden light there always quivers something unresolved, elusively suggestive or mysterious. Rosa was a fierce individualist. Later generations saw him as a proto-Romantic hero, mistakenly thinking him first to have lived among those bandit types he was fond of including in his pictures and then to have joined in Masaniello's populist revolution in Naples in 1647. More concretely his landscapes were imitated both by 18th- and 19th-century painters and landscape architects who saw nature in the same sublime guise, dappled in the light of the imagination.

The final great painter of light in the seventeenth century was, of course, Vermeer, Holland's luminist contemporary to Claude and Rosa in Rome. The use of a camera obscura seems to have helped him see how forms could be dissolved and reconstituted in light. Vermeer infused his incomparable luminosity into genre scenes and rather obvious moralizing allegories, which might have been merely factual in the first case or somewhat pedestrian in the other without this enhancing element. In his absolute command of his craft, Vermeer was the heir to Jan van Eyck and Rogier van der Weyden, the early Netherlandish masters of two centuries before. This concern for and ability to translate into paint the observed light of nature more naturalistically than any other master endowed Vermeer's pictures with that immediacy of intent and technique that reached forward two centuries to the Impressionists.

106

An unearthly group crowds around the Christ Child in Hugo van der Goes' *Adoration of the Shepherds,* central panel of the Portinari Altarpiece, 1475. Uffizi, Florence.

White light of divine significance floods the High Gothic interior of Jan van Eyck's *Madonna in a Church,* ca. 1420. Berlin Museum.

Hieronymus Bosch conveys metaphysical meanings not only in fantastic imagery but also in supraterrestrial color: *The Creation of Eve,* left panel of *The Garden of Delights,* ca. 1500. Prado Museum, Madrid

By Patrik Reuterswärd

What Color Is Divine Light?

To enter the cathedral of Chartres on a sunny day is an unforgettable experience. At first one senses only darkness, which is confusing, as the huge windows indicate a wish to let in as much light as possible. Apparently, the interior light desired was different from that of the square outside. But one need not stay long in the lofty obscurity of the interior to understand the properties of this wished-for light, which, in a way, does not exist until it has passed through the sacred figurations in the stained glass and showered color down to the pillars and the pavement. To be struck by these bundles of prismatic light must have been an overwhelming experience for the medieval mind.

The church was an image of Heaven, the extraordinary nature of which was epitomized by the very *nobilitas* of the materials used. By *nobilitas* was meant that quality of divine light which precious stones and metals as well as stained glass were said to contain to a far greater degree than ordinary materials.[1] In Romanesque churches, large squares of red, blue, yellow and white were painted on pillars and walls in order to simulate precious stones.[2] Gradually, however, this element, so decisive for the whole setting, was taken over by the colored windows which did not just imitate the precious but were in themselves loaded with an utmost degree of *nobilitas*. No wonder that the windows grew larger and finally almost replaced the walls!

Yet the most colorful period of the Gothic is comparatively short. For one thing, the glass became gradually more transparent, allowing more light to pass through, brightening the interiors. To this, however, must be added a growing desire to make the general effect lighter, as is evidenced by the nave of Bourges cathedral, from the end of the 13th century, with its profuse use of white panes in the clerestory windows. But this change towards a lightened effect was not pushed very far, and one may say that the

Patrik Reuterswärd is a Swedish art historian with a special interest in the transition from polychromy to monochromy in Renaissance sculpture. He has taught at the University of Goteborg and in the spring of 1968 was visiting professor at Columbia University. He has now returned to his post as curator at the National Museum, Stockholm, and is completing a work on Hieronymus Bosch.

wish for a colorful shrine of God persisted throughout the 14th century. What a church was supposed to look like in those days is demonstrated by the recently restored church of the Jacobins in Toulouse. The total effect of light is greater than at Chartres, but color is still there, both in the windows and on the walls, and when the sun shines, the interplay of these two systems of decoration creates a divine pattern no less overwhelming than that of Chartres. Again the beholder becomes aware that the light in the church is meant to be totally different from the light outside.

What color and precious materials meant to the 14th century mind is revealed in a eulogy on Paris, composed in 1323 by a professor of philosophy named Jean de Jandun of Senlis. Of his visit to the palace, he lovingly recalls a large table of black marble, which stood in the Great Hall beneath some colored windows, beautifully reflecting at sunset their rays on its dark, polished surface.[3] The passage gives charming evidence of what esthetic refinements delighted an erudite man in those days. Yet these pleasures were nothing compared to the impression which the Ste. Chapelle made on him, with its "exquisite paintings, its images of costly gold, its glistening, radiant windows," etc. Indeed, it was like being "carried off to Heaven and let in to one of Paradise's most beautiful chambers!"[4] We must remember that in those days such a statement was more than mere rhetoric. It was written by a man who had a definite conception of Heaven and who believed in it, too.

However, church interiors were to change considerably. Jan van Eyck's beautiful Berlin Madonna reflects a new attitude; the interior is flooded by a warm light with hardly any spots of color. The transparency of the windows is so great that it has dimmed the power of their colored figures, which do not stain the white bundles of light on the pavement of the church. During the 15th century this warm light was to become cooler and cooler, with the consequence that there was, finally, little difference between the light outside and inside the church.[5] Telling evidence is given by the Master of St. Giles, towards the end of the century, in the way he rendered the interior of St. Denis in his well-known painting in London. Everything is there, or almost everything,[6] depicted with painstaking accuracy: the cross of St. Eloi as well as the 14th-century monument

In Bosch's *Creation of Eve* (detail right; see also p.108), the red face of Christ symbolizes His divinity. Prado Museum, Madrid

Right and detail above: In *The Annunciation* (25⅛ inches high), central panel of the Mérode Altarpiece by Robert Campin (active 1406-1444), the presence of divine illumination in this peaceful interior is expressed by the extinction of the candle and the curling of the book's parchment leaves as if from a sudden heat. Metropolitan Museum, The Cloisters.

The light which floods through the windows in Jan van Eyck's Berlin *Madonna* (detail; see also p.108) is not sunshine since it enters from the north, but light from Heaven.

What Color is Divine Light?

of Dagobert to the right. But the sculptures on the tomb are devoid of their polychromy, of which extensive sections remained long after the picture was painted.[7] And no allusion is made to the stained-glass windows of which Abbot Suger had been so proud. The Master of St. Giles deliberately rendered the daylight of the church as if there were no colored panes in the windows at all.

About 1500 the light inside the Gothic church was thought of virtually as white, despite the fact that stained glass continued to be used.[8] Does this imply a secularization of the church interior, or had the concept of divine light developed towards whiteness? A glance at various phenomena, particularly in Netherlandish painting of the period, may serve to illuminate the question.

Early in the 15th century in the Netherlands, a system for the arrangement of triptychs was established which seems to indicate that the church was no longer that image of Heaven it had been before. The exteriors of the altarpieces were kept grey and monochrome, to contrast with that fullness of color and gold which the opened triptych displayed, usually only on Sundays and feast days.[9] The artists enhanced this contrast by painting simulated statues on the outsides, as if they were seen in the daylight in the church itself, whereas the realm of the opened altar had a light of its own. By this device, the painters implied that the light in the church could only be second to that of the opened altar, where the colors and the gold glistened with the greatest *nobilitas,* creating that sensation of the Extraordinary which previously was evoked by the whole edifice.

Had we only the altarpieces to go by, we could safely maintain that the concept of divine light as something colorful was unchanged in the 15th century, with the only

In *The Miracle of St. Bruno* (detail) by the Master of the
Aachener Schranktüren, ca. 1490, the choir of the church is
flooded in supernatural light. Wallraff-Richartz Museum, Köln.

difference that the realm of the Divine was now confined
to the shrine on the altar. But precious colors and gold
at that stage were perhaps hardly more than conventional
means of expression, and may therefore tell us little of how
contemporaneous minds felt about Divine Light. It is one
of the great centuries of transition, and we should not be
surprised also to find other means for expressing this metaphysical quality.

To moderns, Divine Light if describable at all, should be
something similar to yet far more brilliant and resplendent
than physical light. That this reasoning was already present
in the 15th century is evidenced by Jan van Eyck's Berlin
Madonna, the secret of which has been so ingeniously revealed by the late Erwin Panofsky.[10] Having secularized the
church by letting in white, terrestrial light, the painter
needed a device for expressing its divine significance, and he
achieved this simply by changing the direction of the sunshine, which in the picture floods down from the north
instead of from the south. Had he placed the Virgin in the
somber twilight of Chartres, surrounded by prismatic spots
of colored light, he would hardly have needed such an
irrational device, but to van Eyck, as to many in his time,
the true nature of Divine Light had to be expressed in terms
of intensity rather than hue. It was something which outdid
ordinary light through elimination and difference (as did
indeed the penumbra of Chartres), and yet it was expressive
through its resplendence, not to say whiteness.

Even though the painters became gradually aware of the
impossibility of representing Divine Light, they were, nevertheless, impelled to find visual forms for its nature. The
safest way, of course, was to leave it out, and simply to
concentrate on the effects of its presence. In the Mérode

Blue light is the attribute of divinity in *The Transfiguration of Christ*, page from the Byzantine ms. of John Cantacuzenos, 1370-75. Bibliothèque Nationale, Paris.

114

What Color is Divine Light?

Altarpiece, the Master of Flémalle, Robert Campin, has expressed this negative presence by blowing out the candle on the table beside the Virgin. From its wick rises a beautiful curl of smoke, which tells us that it was snuffed out just a second ago. Moreover, on the table next to it lies an opened manuscript with its parchment leaves curled, as though suddenly exposed to heat or sunshine.

Since this picture has already been subject to so many interpretations,[11] one hesitates before offering a solution of one's own. However, most writers seem to agree that the cause of these disturbances in the peaceful chamber of the Virgin is the sudden presence of a Light which is stronger than terrestrial light, whoever brought it into the room. Has it come with the Angel Gabriel, or is it the arrival of the nude Christ Child by the window which has so suddenly extinguished the candle? I believe that neither of these forces, however divine, is actually the agent of this power, nor is it to be understood as invisibly omnipresent in the room. It may not even be there any longer. All that the picture tells is that it was there a moment ago! However, something more is missing, and I believe this may offer the final clue: the Dove of the Holy Spirit, which, according to the widely read *Meditationes* of Pseudo-Bonaventura, arrived first and entered the Virgin before the Infant: the Spirit came over her "like a divine fire, inflaming the mind and sanctifying the flesh with the most perfect purity. Thus the virtue of the Most High was infused into her in order that she might be able to sustain such ardor".[12] In the picture we see the Christ Child arriving in a golden stream of "ardor," but the candle's curl of smoke seems to indicate, in its discreet way, that the Holy Spirit has in fact passed just a moment ago and entered the Virgin—on its way extinguishing the flame of the candle and, by virtue of being a divine "fire," curling the parchment leaves of the manuscript on the table.[13]

We must admire Robert Campin's ability to conceal the appearance of divine matter and yet give an idea of its supernatural qualities. But when introducing the Christ Child, he could not avoid the problem of representation by simply eliminating Divine Light. He therefore resorted to the traditional device of adding rays of gold. Since time immemorial, gold, the only material which never changes, had been used to signify the divine.[14] It is often difficult to tell whether it stands for a realm of light or for a divine fire, like the halo, which had made its appearance by Homeric times and seems to imply both. That Divine Light was thought of as fire as well becomes all the more evident when we view Robert Campin's *Nativity* in Dijon. On the ground lies the Infant Christ emitting faint rays of gold; they stand for a light which, according to St. Bridget, was so strong that it annihilated terrestrial light; therefore Joseph has to protect the candle-flame with his hand.[15] But in order to explain the nature of this divine power, the painter added, as a reminder, an apocryphal story about the two midwives. The legend tells that one of them, Salome, had

mistrusted the virginity of the Virgin, but when the time of birth approached and Salome assisted at the delivery, her hand was consumed by divine fire in the Virgin's womb.

In much the same way, the analogy of the Burning Bush[16] served to emphasize the firelike nature of the Divine Embryo, a quality for which gold long remained the most adequate means of expression; and gold for long had been the only acceptable material for the halo, the radiance of the Christ Child. Towards the end of the 15th century, however, Geertgen tot Sint Jans ingeniously applied artificial light as a substitute for the gold: in his charming *Nativity* in London, the Christ Child and the Angel appearing to the shepherds are the only two sources of light of the nocturnal scene.[17] Once established, this mode of representation proved highly effective, all the more so as the warm tone suggested both ardor and extraordinary brilliancy.

Hugo van der Goes had experimented before Geertgen with a seemingly normal light radiating from the Christ Child, but he combined it with the rays of traditional gold. His solution was, nevertheless, more dynamic than that of his contemporaries—as the Infant lies in the center of the enormous Portinari Altarpiece, one feels that He is the agent of supernatural powers. The surrounding space is empty, in an almost nuclear way, and there is something strange about the whole arrangement, with small angels contrasting with large shepherds bending before the tiny and yet almighty Creature. This dynamic system of representation was continued by Matthias Grünewald in his great vision of the Resurrected Christ in the Isenheim Altarpiece. The head of the Saviour is surrounded by a huge reddish halo, which gradually turns yellow towards its divine center. To speak here only of light would be misleading, since the whole picture gives the impression of an explosion: the guards of the grave seem to have been slung away by the light of the rising Christ. By this time, the effects of gunpowder were well known, and not only blacksmiths understood that there is an almost blue-white zone in the center of a fire, where the heat is greatest. Grünewald no doubt based his vision not only on observations of light [see Cover]; in fact this extraordinary epiphany might better be described in terms of lightning.[18]

The "lightning" epiphany has been ever since the main type of naturalistic representation of Divine Light. Grünewald's vision comprises both a dynamic note and one which is silent and calm—in the center of the light everything stands still, as it actually does in the center of a storm. This calm side was monumentalized by Rembrandt, who has given the most sublime solutions to a naturalistic rendering of the divine. The angel appearing to Christ on the Mount of Olives as well as Christ himself in His greatest moments of revelation—to Rembrandt, such manifestations of godship could only be visualized in terms of a vast silent flash of lightning, and he did it in such a natural, self-evident way that even unbelievers may believe.

Yet the painters and their patrons had long been aware of the limitations of naturalistic rendering. Ever since Jan

The interior of St.-Denis depicted in *The Mass of St. Giles,* ca. 1480 (National Gallery, London), is rendered in everyday light, without allusion to the Abbot Suger's vaunted stained-glass windows (see p.42).

What Color is Divine Light?

van Eyck (not to mention the men behind Chartres), those who were deeply concerned knew that the Divine can only be expressed in terms of differences. An interesting case is Hieronymus Bosch and his contradictory attitude toward the problem. In his early works, as well as in his very late ones, he painted a cross of rays around the head of the Saviour, but during his long mature period, he used far less traditional means for this purpose. In the *Haywain* and in the *Last Judgment* in Vienna, both God the Father and Christ are surrounded by a yellowish light instead of gold. And in

Gold rays from the Christ Child in Robert Campin's *Nativity*, ca. 1420,
expresses illumination more brilliant than the light of day. Musée Magnin, Dijon.

The actual source of light in Geertgen tot Sint Jans' *Nativity,* ca. 1490, is the Christ Child himself, with a secondary illumination from the angel appearing to the shepherds. National Gallery, London.

In the Master of the Legend of St. Ursula's *Dream of the Saint,* ca. 1580, the scene is simply illuminated by the radiance of the angel. Wallraf-Richartz Museum, Köln.

What Color is Divine Light?

his most sublime vision of Heaven, that which we glimpse through a large tunnel in one of his After Life panels in Venice, Heaven is nothing but a warm white light.

There is only one instance of a halo in the master's mature period, namely in the *Temptations of St. Anthony* in Lisbon, where Christ wears it while appearing to the saint. But Bosch seems to have done this mainly for the sake of St. Anthony and because the legend expressly prescribed an epiphany. And he even added that very light with which Christ, according to the text, had descended to Earth—a few yards away,

a misty ray operates almost like a laser-beam, as though waiting to take Him back to Heaven.

For the rest, Bosch avoided halos and rays. He had a Netherlandish tradition to rely on here, but the interesting point is that he was not always satisfied with this negative solution either. As long as holiness could be indicated by expression alone, there was no need for halos. In Bosch's close-ups of the mocked Saviour, in London and at the Escorial, Christ has become God by his very humanity. But on other occasions, such as when Christ unites Adam and

Eve in the Garden of Eden in the so-called *Garden of Delights,* the painter felt a need of emphasizing His commanding greatness as a Being beyond other beings. The device which he used to this end is quite remarkable: he reinstated divinity simply by giving Christ a reddish complexion.

Bosch had done the same to St. Agnes in the right panel of the Prado *Epiphany,* and probably the blushing face of his St. John the Baptist in Madrid is likewise meant to express godhead. This leads me to make a short comment on red as a connotation of the divine. Its motivations are very much the same as those of a golden halo, and yet there must have been a difference. As a common denominator stands the idea of the divine as something out of the ordinary. Already in ancient Egypt, the epiphany of the deity had been described in terms of extraordinary brightness and color, [19] and later great heros, such as Alexander, were recognized by their fiery complexion. [20] This reddish appearance went along with other signs, such as the golden hair and the aura which subsequently became the Christian halo. In Early Christian mosaics, the angels wear not only halos but have fiery red faces, [21] and in the case of representations of the Angel at the grave of Christ, this practice can be traced throughout the medieval period. [22] The red hue of the angel refers expressly to the wording of the Gospel: "And his face was like lightning" (Matthew, 28:3). As long as red was the color of fire, this particular angel was to be represented red, and in France this convention was in force throughout the 15th century, [23] i.e., even after the painters had found new formulas for the representation of fire.

Since other angels of consequence, including the archangel Gabriel of the Annunciation, hardly ever appear with fiery complexions, [24] we could conclude that red was used only where the text prescribed a resemblance to fire and lightning. [25] As for Bosch, we would thus assume that he alluded to the fiery nature of the divine when giving Christ a reddish face. In other words, this device would have meant to him much the same as did the golden rays of the Infant Christ to the Master of Flémalle. However, the red hue may also point in a different direction. Even though church fathers, including Origenes and St. Augustine, had claimed the fiery nature of angels, the red hue was in those times also seen as an expression of the Spirit, *pnevma;* [26] which

What Color is Divine Light?

Lying in the center of the Portinari Altarpiece (detail, see also p.108), the Christ Child emanating rays of gold appears as the agent of supernatural powers. Uffizi, Florence.

should suggest an aerial connotation as well. And certainly something of this kind was also felt in the 15th century—how else can we explain those red zones of angels which frame the golden Heavens of that time? Yet, beyond this red angelical zone of the Seraphim, there usually followed the blue realm of the Cherubim which, by its color and outer location, suggests a greater kinship with the terrestial atmosphere. Judging from the pictures alone, one would thus propose that the red Seraphim held a position between the eternal fiery gold and the aerial blue of the Cherubim. But there were differences in meaning, too: according to some writers, the red angels were burning with divine Love, whereas the blue angels were radiant with divine Knowledge.[27] These meanings may however have been developed only as afterthoughts.

Now, in the case of Bosch, it is not just an angel but the most Supreme Deity which appears red. In this the painter was preceded only by Rogier van der Weyden, who had God the Father appear as if made of a translucid red substance when sending out the Holy Spirit of Baptism.[28] Whatever this substance was meant to imply, Rogier's God the Father seems imbued by a red light very much like that of a sunset. This leads us back again to late antiquity, where Servius, commenting on the 6th Eclogue of Vergil, reveals that many at that time believed that the gods were red.[29] And when discussing the red-faced Pan of the 10th Eclogue, he continued: "Pan painted his face *"propter aetheris similitudinem,"* i.e., "in order to resemble the upper air," adding the sublime lapidary remark: *aether autem est Jupiter.*[30]

This text was known to Signorelli, who alluded to it when giving the sky behind his great Pan a bright copper tone. There the almighty Pan, himself a deep brownish hue, is sitting with his pensive companions against an evening sky which is intended to remind us of Pan's identity with the Great Only God. The painting was destroyed in the flames of Berlin in 1945, and can be seen today only in black-and-white reproductions, which unfortunately do not transmit the significance of the sky.

Signorelli's great painting proves that these pagan thoughts were known to the Humanists in Florence. We should not, however, underestimate the erudition of the Northerners either. They, too, were well acquainted with ancient scripture on Pan, as may be evidenced by a French manuscript illustration which shows Pan with all his characteristics: the red face, the horns, the stars, the trestle-leg, and the many-piped flute. However droll, this merry Pan is rendered correctly by a painter who knew little or nothing of pagan statuary and yet everything essential as far as textual evidence goes. Speaking of Bosch, who was the starting point of this *excursus*, I have the impression that he, too, knew a great deal of ancient speculation. We know for certain, at least, that he was familiar with pagan gems.[31]

A discussion of divine light cannot be closed without a glance at the blue sphere as well. Judging from the way this occurs in 15th-century painting, we may conclude that it was usually considered as secondary to the red. Yet there is an instance where the blue realm appears as the foremost, and, again, the example is from Bosch. In one of his early works, the table-top with the Seven Deadly Sins in the Prado, Christ appears as the very center of a sun. He is surrounded by a brim of gold which, in its turn, sends out a golden aura which gradually turns into a delicate peach-red color, as do the 127 concentric rays as well.[32] The affinity

A representation of the pagan god Pan in a 14th-century ms. illumination closely follows classical literary sources, including a red face as an attribute of divinity. Bibliothèque Nationale, Paris.

between gold and red could hardly have been expressed more exquisitely. Yet, instead of adding a blue zone to the red periphery, Bosch rendered the very center of this sun blue: Christ appears there rising from his tomb against a blue background. Instead of the usual stratification gold-red-blue, we thus get one which proceeds from a blue core.

Bosch must have known of certain conventions which justified blue as the color of the Most High. In Early Christian times, when gold was the most perfect expression for the Divine, there were, nevertheless, instances where the golden realm gave way to something blue beyond. Surrounded by a blue atmosphere, God's hand could suddenly interfere in the golden narrative of the mosaics, and in the baptisteries the golden dome opened, like the Pantheon's, at its vertex to a blue sky, which had a representation of the Baptism of Christ. This tradition of a divine blue matter which, on occasion, might even outdo the realm of gold, was carried on by the Eastern Church, where it became particularly apparent in representations of the Transfiguration of Christ. While the church fathers went on discussing, over and over again, the true nature of Christ at this miraculous incident, the painters, too, did their best to make His nature clear. They seem to have decided that the most adequate solution was to give Christ a blue halo and to show Him sending out three broad rays of the blue down to the wonder-struck disciples.

To conclude, let us listen to Gregory Palamas, one of those learned holy men who in the 14th century fervently continued the debate on the Transfiguration. "God is called Light," he says, "not so much for His spirit, or essence, as for His very energy."[33] That miraculous light which appeared to the three disciples below was nothing that could be experienced by the senses, nor was it, to Gregory, to be understood as something purely conceptual. Rather he would describe it by way of a paradox as a Light which "has never begun and will never cease." Perceiving it presupposes a transfiguration of the beholder as well, a grace which the Lord has bestowed only upon His disciples who, however, could bear it only a short moment, because the brilliancy of His "light cloud" totally surpassed their powers of perception. Christ became rapidly invisible to them, and they fell down with fear.

Here not only Grünewald's *Resurrection* comes to mind. This pious exposition of a theophany is based on a vast number of testimonies to the Divine Energy, beginning with Salome's experience of the Divine as something fire-like. Even though gold and red remained the most effective means of expression for this fiery quality, we may certainly understand those Byzantine and Russian painters who, when it came to the Transfiguration, preferred blue. By doing so, they underlined the incommensurability of the light of Christ. Gold, however sacred, was avoided simply because it resembled physical light too much. We must remember that the Divine had to be expressed in terms of difference rather than in terms of analogy and likeness. Difference, in

The large sun behind the Saviour in *The Resurrection* by Thomas von Klausenburg, ca. 1427, prefigures Grünewald's stupendous halo (see cover). Christian Museum, Esztergom, Hungary.

Christ appears in a blue
oculus at the center of a sun in
Bosch's *Seven Deadly Sins* (detail),
ca. 1475-80. Prado, Madrid.

fact, has been the main principle in the Christian East as well as at Chartres in the West, and at all periods—from Early Christian times down to van Eyck and Bosch.

1. According to a treatise called *Liber de intelligentiis*, written towards the middle of the 13th century, probably in Paris. See W. Schöne, *Uber das Licht in der Malerei*, Berlin 1954, p. 66.
2. Remains of this Romanesque system of decoration can be found in numerous churches, e.g. in the nave of St. Sernin, Toulouse.
3. *Eloge de Paris, composé en 1323 par un habitant de Senlis, Jean de Jandun, publié pour la première fois par MM. Taranne et Le*

Roux de Lincy, Bulletin du Comité de la langue, de l'histoire et des arts de la France, III, 1857, p. 518: *Sed et marmorea mensa, sue politissime planitiei uniformitate refulgens, sub occidentalium vitrearum lumine fixa, sic tamen quod ad oriens respiciunt convivantes, tante profecto magnitudinis existit quod si mensuram ejus absque probatione proponerem, timerem michi non credi.*
4. *Ibid., p. 517: Picturarum colores electissimi, ymaginum deauratis preciosa, vitrearum circumquaque rutilantium decora pervietas, altarium venustissima paramenta, sanctuariorum virtutes mirifice, capsularum figurationes extranee gemmis adornate fulgentibus, tantam utique illi orationis domui largiuntur decoris yperbolem ut, in eam*

What Color is Divine Light?

Two panels from a diptych of *The Last Judgment* by Hieronymus Bosch, ca. 1495, Doge's Palace, Venice.

Above left: In the *Ascension of Souls to Paradise,* the light from Heaven is glimpsed through a long tunnel. **Right:** In *Souls in Paradise,* the Elect raise their eyes to the light of God.

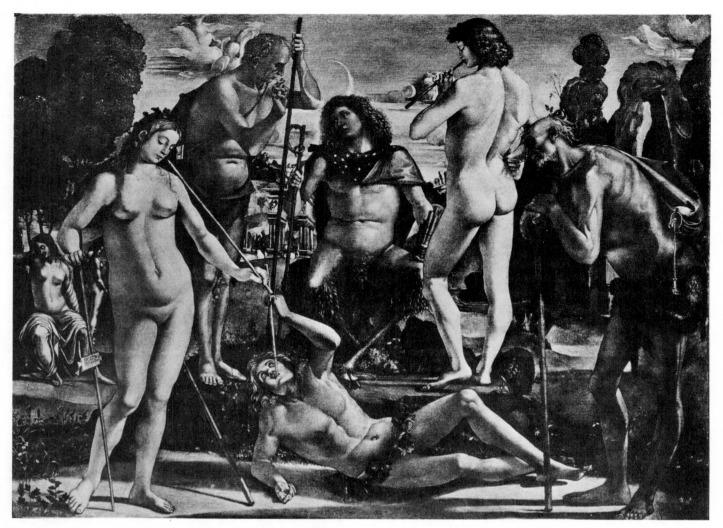

Impregnated with Neo-Platonic symbolism, Signorelli's *Education of Pan* distinguishes the god from his companions by his brownish hue. Formerly in the Berlin Museum, this famous work painted in 1488-90 for Lorenzo de' Medici was destroyed by fire in World War II.

subingrediens, quasi raptus ad celum, se non immerito unam de paradisi potissimis cameris putet intrare.

5. From the middle of the century we have Rogier van der Weyden's testimony, as given in his Altar of the Seven Sacraments, Antwerp, with its totally grey interior and whitish light. It is said to show the interior of St. Gudule, Brussels, though Rogier's forms are far more elongated and slender. The painter probably idealized the light as well. There is also an extraordinary painting by the Master of the "Aachener Schranktüren" from about 1490, which should not be overlooked either. The painting, now in Cologne, shows a Romanesque nave to which has been added a Gothic choir which is virtually flooded in a white light. See A.Stange, *Deutsche Malerei der Gotik*, 5, 1952, Fig. 114.

6. As has been shown by W.Hinkle, "The Iconography of the Four Panels of the Master of Saint Giles," *Journal of the Warburg and Courtauld Institutes*, 28, 1965, pp. 110ff., the painter made certain adjustments as to the selection of sacred objects.

7. Even at the beginning of the 19th century there were extensive remains of the ancient polychromy. See P.Vitry & G.Brière, *L'Eglise abbatiale de Saint-Denis*, Paris 1908, p.111, and A.Lenoir, *Monuments des arts libéraux*, etc., 1840, p. 29.

8. And not many missed the old somber interiors. P.Frankl, *The*

Gothic, Princeton 1960, pp. 219f., reports of a monk named Niavis, who describes the old church of Annaberg as "a strongly built but old-fashioned building and not light, because people formerly thought that it encouraged religious fervor when a church was not too light."

9. With the exception of the period of Lent, when the triptychs were always closed. See M. Teasdale Smith, "The Use of Grisaille as a Lenten Observance," *Marsyas*, 8, 1959, pp. 43ff.

10. E.Panofsky, *Early Netherlandish Painting*, Cambridge, Mass., 1953, pp. 147f.

11. A whole book is being written on the Mérode Altarpiece, by Charles L.Minott, Philadelphia, and it is to be hoped that it will include a full bibliography on the subject.

12. David M.Robb, "The Iconography of the Annunciation in the Fourteenth and Fifteenth Centuries," *Art Bulletin*, 18, 1936, p. 524.

13. I offered this solution at Columbia University last year. After the lecture, one of my students, Donald W.Powell, made a very suggestive remark, which I wish to communicate here. He noted that the marked white highlights on the lap of the Virgin form a starlike pattern—I would even say, the shape of a fluttering dove. Did the painter, too, calculate this observation?

14. See P.Reuterswärd, *Studien zur Polychromie der Plastik. I. Agyp-*

ten, Stockholm 1958, pp. 18ff., and *II. Griechenland und Rom,* 1960, pp. 143ff.

15. Panofsky, *op.cit.,* pp. 126, 158.

16. See E.M. Vetter, *"Maria im brennenden Dornbusch," Das Münster,* 10, 1957, pp.237ff.

17. Another beautiful specimen is offered by the Master of the Legend of St. Ursula, in his panel showing the angel appearing to the saint, Cologne. See W.R.Deusch, *Deutsche Malerei des 15. Jahrhunderts,* Berlin 1936, pl. 77. To the Italians, on the other hand, this way of representing divine light as just light was nothing new: A classical example is Taddeo Gaddi's representation of the angel appearing to the shepherds, in the Baroncelli Chapel, Sta. Croce, Florence.

18. The stage before Grünewald is best illustrated by a Resurrection in Esztergom, Hungary, which was painted about 1427 by a gifted Siebenbürgen painter named Thomas von Klausenburg. The large sun behind the Saviour prefigures by its size Grunewald's stupendous halo, but the dynamic note of the latter's vision is absent. Still, the miracle of the Resurrection remains even more of a miracle here, since Christ rises from His sealed grave without removing the covering stone slab. This type of representation was more or less introduced by the Master of Wittingau and then occurred frequently throughout the 15th century (for a sample of German specimens, see A.Stange, *Deutsche Malerei der Gotik,* 2:61; 3:50, 74, and 85; 4:93, 95, and 226; 5:62, and 156; 6:38, and 252; 7:138; 8:215; 10:57; 11:24, 279, 321, and 326). In Grünewald's time the sealed-grave type of representation was combined with extraordinary light effects by Jörg Ratgeb in his Herrenberg Altarpiece in Stuttgart. Besides having a halo as large as Grünewald's, Ratgeb's Christ sends out light from His five wounds as well. For a reproduction, see W.Fraenger, in *Castrum Peregrini,* 29, 1956.

19. There is a charming fragment of a pastoral story where a shepherd, taken aback by the appearance of a great goddess, exclaims: "Her color was so gay that it made my hair stand on end." See Erman, *Literatur der Aegypter,* 1923, p.63.

20. Reuterswärd, *op.cit.,* 1960, pp. 198f. As for Alexander, note also his dark, fiery appearance in the famous mosaic in Naples.

21. E.g., the representation of Abraham entertaining the three Angels, in Sta. Maria Maggiore, Rome.

22. To give a complete list is impossible. Here are a few specimens which I once recorded in the Staatsbibliothek at Munich: Cod. lat. 15903, fol. 39r (from Salzburg, 12th c.), 3900, fol. 81v (from Augsburg, 13th c.), 11308, fol. 10r (from Polling, 13th c.), and 835, fol. 26v (English, 13th c.).

23. Paris, Bibl.nat., Ms. fr. 179, fol. 194, and Munich, Cod. iconogr. 414, fol. 13r, both in the manner of Jean Colombe.

24. Red well suited the fierce angel of the Expulsion, as can be seen in Masaccio's famous fresco.

25. The most conspicious case should have been the Transfiguration of Christ (Matthew, 17:2: "And His face shone like the sun"). However, I have only recorded one representation where Christ accordingly appears with a red face, namely in a manuscript from the 1430s in Munich (Cod. Germ. 8010), by a most original illuminator named Martinus Opifex. See A.Stange, *op.cit.,* 11:75. As will be discussed below, Byzantine and Russian painters preferred blue in their representations of the Transfiguration. On the other hand, they painted Elijah's sun-chariot red.

26. E.Kirschbaum, *"L'Angelo rosso e l'angelo turchino," Rivista di archeologia cristiana,* 1940, pp.213f.

27. *Ibidem,* pp.234ff. Rather intriguing is a detail in Rogier van der Weyden's Beaune Altarpiece which Dr. Th. Feder, New York, has kindly pointed out to me. Behind the Gates of Heaven one sees a crowd of red beings which do not seem to be angels. Maybe they represent blessed souls.

28. In the St.John triptychs in Berlin and Frankfort. I have only seen the latter, but I believe this observation is also applicable to the version in Berlin.

29. Commentary to line 22: *multi ob hoc dictum putant, quod robeus colorum deorum sit.*

30. Commentary to line 27: *facie rubra pingitur Pan propter aetheris similitudinem: aether autem est Iuppiter.*

31. J.Baltrusaitis, *Le moyen-âge fantastique,* Paris 1955, p.62, has fully proved that Bosch utilized figures from antique gems for his fantastic flying and floating vessels in the *Temptation of St.Anthony* in Lisbon. As Dr. Marian Wenzel-Evans, London, has pointed out to me, the large central figures of the so-called *Garden of Delights* also must rely on classical gems.

32. The *rays* were counted by W.Fraenger, *"Hieronymus Bosch: Der Tisch der Weisheit, bisher 'Die sieben Todsünden' genannt," Psyche* 5, 1951, pp. 355ff., who attached a deep Pythagorean significance to their number.

33. I follow here the German version given by W.Lossky in Ouspensky & Lossky, *Der Sinn der Ikonen,* Berne 1952, p.211: *"Gott wird Licht genannt nicht nach Seinem Wesen, sondern nach Seiner Energie."*

Proto-psychedelic light-extravaganza:
J. Besoet's *Fireworks in an Outdoor Theater, The Hague,*
engraving, 1749. Gemeente Museum, The Hague.

By John Perreault

Literal Light

A yellow smoky light?
A corrosive light?
A candid light?
A flattering light?

Light given off by rhodochrosite if a rhodochrosite gives off light. Enter a chorus of grumbling priests carrying magnesium flares and hoes.   Jackson MacLow, *Light Poems*

Also the writer remembers back a few years when during a lecture Marshall McLuhan pointed to a glowing light bulb and remarked that it radiated pure information—at least to those who understood its signal. Increasingly pure energy and information seem to be the essences of art: all else is being dropped methodically by the wayside.
Jack Burnham, *Beyond Modern Sculpture*

& the light of questionable-motivation-finding &
other unfriendly lights
on this simple act
that I can
see in this affirmative light
as merely your attempt to throw
the light of your critical insight
on this "bad try" of mine
at showing a superior trait of some of my neighbors
in the objective & admiring light
I think it deserves?   Jackson MacLow, *Light Poems*

More light!   Goethe, on his deathbed

We have been witnessing of late attempts to effect a "dematerialization" of art. Advanced art is advanced by virtue of its concern with process, concepts, systems and energy. To speak of new art in terms of art objects has become increasingly difficult. Even those works that maintain a foothold on materiality and achieve their effects by way of some measurable object are usually of interest not because of the way the object looks, but because of the situation the object

John Perreault is well known both as a poet and as the author of a lively art column which appears weekly in New York's *Village Voice*. Last summer he taught at the Writer's Workshop of the University of Iowa.

creates for the receiver of the information it transmits, optically and kinesthetically.

More and more we are best able to understand the universe in terms of fields of energy. We may see the world as full of objects, but our knowledge penetrates this familiar world of hard entities. Matter when scrutinized dematerializes into waves and/or particles: sheer energy. The most obvious and most visible kind of energy we are familiar with is, of course, light.

Who as a child has not used a prism to break up light into rainbows, or a magnifying glass to start a fire, or a pocket-mirror as a "ray-gun" to wage war against interplanetary interlopers?

The sun is a universal symbol of energy, both spiritual and physical. Even we post-moderns worship light on grimy beaches, on the edges of turquoise swimming pools, from coast to coast and around the world, in search of the ultimate sun-tan. We offer ourselves as burnt sacrifices to that blinding, carcinogenic light. We lie prostrate and naked before a religious symbol as old as man. As the inner light retreats, the outer light is increasingly courted.

On the other hand, artificial light has become so familiar that we hardly notice it at all. We need regional power failures every so often to dramatize how much we take electric light for granted and how we have become dependent upon it. With the electric light we have changed the "natural" order of things ("early to bed and early to rise") and created for ourselves the proper light to change our time schedules at will or by whim, leaving other contingencies, such as work-routines and play-routines (what ironies are contained within the latter formulation!) to govern our divisions of the hours. We have created whole cities inhabited by night owls. Through the gift of the electric light one can seek one's dole of peaceful silence further and further beyond the "midnight oil," until day becomes night and night becomes day and one finds that callers at noon are prefacing their business with apologies for disturbing one's sleep.

Our cities at night, when darkness shields us from the grime and the debris, are transformed into stacks of geometrical Christmas trees, rendering unto Caesar what is Caesar's. But how rarely do we notice these everyday lights

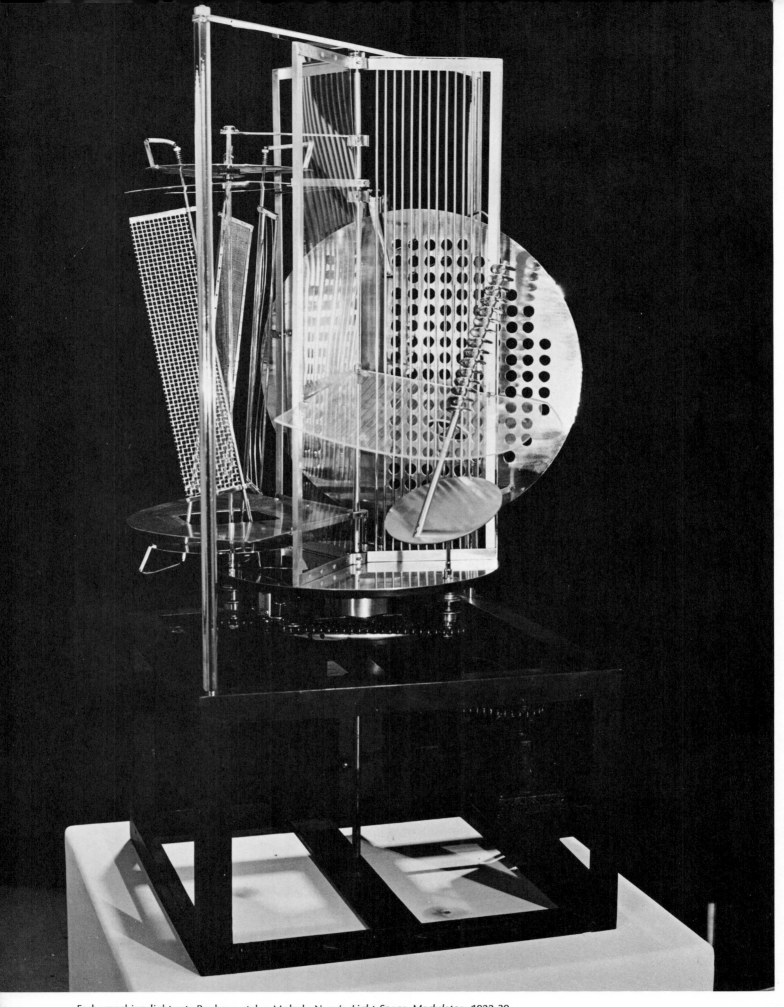

Early machine-light-art, Bauhaus style: Moholy-Nagy's *Light-Space Modulator,* 1922-30, steel, plastics and wood, 59½ inches high. Busch-Reisinger Museum, Harvard University.

that surround us. We notice light most when a bulb burns out, when a fluorescent begins to flicker, or when, armed with an electric shaver, we squint at ourselves in a mirror beneath this very same fluorescent and wonder where the colors went and curse the vampire, color-draining light.

One extremely valuable, but needless to say limited, view claims that art is a tool of perception, that it is an instrument fashioned to increase our awareness. This may fly in the face of "art-for-art's sake" dictums, but nevertheless provides some helpful hints when dealing with new kinds of art that are ephemeral, disposable, theatrical or immaterial. Art need not only be for contemplation. Another kind of art can and does exist. Once we have received the information it imparts and new connections have been made between a few of our brain cells we feel free to walk away from it, or sell it to the highest bidder, or throw it away.

We need never even own it. Certainly artificial light, so much a part of our environment—light *is* our environment —could use some pointing out, some framing.

The first esthetic use of man-made light probably involved the use of fire in some dim, dark paeleolithic cave. (Yves Klein's *Fire Fountains* are one modern example of the use of fire.) One of the oldest forms of Light Art, however, is not only one of the purest, but is also one of the most popular. Fireworks are to this day universally admired and occasion a sense of delight even in the most sophisticated.

So rare is the direct use of natural light in contemporary art (I can think of but one example: Charles Ross's excellent Plexiglas, mineral-oil-filled prisms that scatter rainbows into the environment) that for all practical purposes we can assume that when we are talking about Light Art we are talking about man-made light. Of course, under the heading

Two phases of Thomas Wilfred's Lumia composition, *Aspiration, Op. 145,* 1955, projected light on plexiglas screen, 19¼ inches high. The sequence lasts about 42¼ hours. Museum of Modern Art, New York.

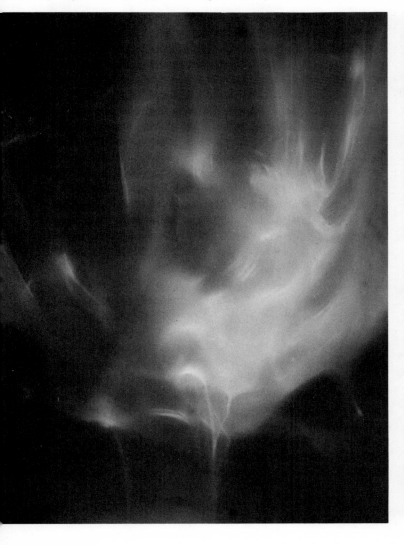 

"Natural Light" one might include older examples, such as stained glass windows, the use of sun-reflecting metals on the outsides of buildings, the faceting of precious stones to catch and amplify the sun's rays. A Siamese temple or an engagement ring might both be looked upon as static "light machines."

In modern times the advent of electricity should have made possible an entirely new art form, for here for the first time with electricity was a light source that could be easily molded by the hand and the mind of the artist. Moholy-Nagy and other sages of the Bauhaus were enthusiastic, perpetually. But the attempts at Light Art—even Moholy-Nagy's *Light-Space Modulator* or, in America, Thomas Wilfred's *Lumia*—in retrospect seem inadequate and uninspiring.

Why have we had to wait until recently to get our first inklings of Light Art as a really new form? The possibilities

of pure, direct light were never fully grasped. Moholy-Nagy's *Modulator* and Wilfred's *Lumia,* although these historically important works continue to be imitated right down to the present moment, utilize a potentially new medium to imitate an old one, namely painting. The addition of time elements only compounds the error, because it was obvious from the beginning that the cinema can deal with time much more efficiently and effectively, particularly in terms of the effects created by these two works. What we are now interested in is light itself and the specific properties of this most immaterial of "new" materials.

The idea of using light projected from behind onto a translucent screen is not new. We can go back to the 18th century and to Luis-Bertrand Castel's "ocular harpsichord," which attempted a marriage between sound and light, a mistake repeated over and over again and not rectified

Two versions of Chryssa's boxed neon sculptures, ca. 1966 and 1967, offshoots of a much larger work, *The Gates to Times Square*. The one at right is cased in deeply smoked plastic and appears empty when the light is off. Pace Gallery.

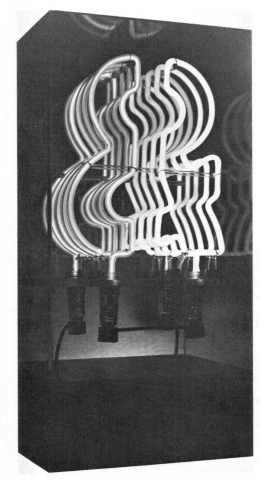

Dan Flavin's space-altering light system composed of equal 8-foot fluorescent tubes: *Pink and Gold,* 1969, at the Museum of Contemporary Art, Chicago.

Stephen Antonakos: *Walk-On Neon*, 1968, 9-by-12 foot platform with programmed neon panels under heavy plexiglas, with an exposed free-standing diagonal in the center. Fischbach Gallery.

until Thomas Wilfred, who—to pay him his due—insisted that the shifting, smoky, pastel forms of his *Lumia* could stand on their own and should not be violated by musical or sound accompaniment. Light Shows such as now accompany rock-and-roll performances, although often hypnotic and quite decorative, must be seen as a retreat if one insists upon treating them as serious art. However, they are often an improvement over Walt Disney's atrocious Mickey-Mousing of Bach in *Fantasia,* possibly because they are improvised to live music by people who have some feeling for the music involved.

By now we can see that the use of light as an art material is not entirely new. What is new is the use of literal light, light used for its own sake. Light Art at its best is as different from sculpture as sculpture is from painting. Under the general heading of Light Art, many forms can be listed, varying in degrees of purity. Taking into consideration the embarrassing fact that purity in art is not necessarily a virtue (nor is it in life, for that matter), it will still be safe to assume—at least as we begin to emerge from a long period of artistic unconsciousness in regards to what can be considered one of the 20th century's really new materials—that purity—here meaning the literal use of light—is of some esthetic relevance. It is certainly therapeutic.

Although the pun implicit in the term Light Art is unfortunate (there is still much truth in it), no other name seems

Les Levine: *Standard Equipment,* 1969, light environment at the U.C.L.A. galleries. U-shaped fluorescent tubes are suspended from the ceiling in an 8-foot square. Fischbach Gallery.

so efficient. Light Art may most generally be defined as an art form that uses light as its main "material." Light Art that uses light, not only as its main "material," but as its subject as well, I consider to be "literal light" and the best and most advanced kind of Light Art within the category.

As interesting as some works are that incorporate light and light fixtures as one aspect of a conglomeration of images or objects—Larry Rivers's *Lampman*, some works of Robert Rauschenberg and of George Segal—since light is not the main "material" used, they cannot really be considered in the category.

Cinema and television may be indeed thought of as a sub-class of Light Art, but so highly developed have they become as art forms that their category would be much, much larger and often much more interesting and relevant than other forms of Light Art, engulfing more delicate propositions. Artists have long used films. The list is long: Duchamp, Man Ray, Hans Richter, right up into the present, with excellent short films being made by artists as divergent in outlook as Bruce Conner and Richard Serra. One cannot except Andy Warhol whose film *Empire* is a brilliant but monotonous celebration of the lights of the Empire State Building. Television also is being utilized as a medium by artists. Bruce Nauman shows video tapes as does Les Levine, whose multiple-tube television pieces *Iris* and *Contact* exploit both the medium and viewer participation via closed-circuit set-ups. The purist use of film in terms of Light Art is Tony Conrad's *Flick*, which through programmed alterna-

tions between "white" and "dark" frames creates strobe effects. The only pure use of television that I know of—we must, I am afraid, leave out Nam June Paik's very witty magnetic distortions of broadcast images, but perhaps his abstract images might qualify if we stretched our definitions a bit—is poet Hannah Weiner's *Guns of Will Sonnet*, a theater work in which the audience is treated to ten minutes of beautiful (but, to some, infuriating) blue flicker projected without sound on an empty stage by a portable television set, placed with its back to the audience.

There are already two traditional distinctions made within Light Art: indirect light (projected and reflected light) and direct. Indirect light includes not only the cinema, but also the kinds of effects obtained by artists such as Julio Le Parc or Nicholas Schöffer by means of reflecting light off of highly polished sheets of metal, often in motion. One of the best and purest examples of projected light I know of are the light rectangles of James Turrell, a West Coast artist who projects high-intensity light directly on bare walls. One also needs to mention Robert Whitman's splendid use of the laser beam in his piece called *Dark*, in which a ruby-red line traced and retraced itself around the walls of a darkened gallery. Other exceptional projected works utilize what might be called the "searchlight effect." Forrest Myers directed four searchlights into the sky above Tompkins Square Park in New York. More recently Marvin Torffield's *Interfusion* at the Jewish Museum consisted of various light beams projected into a vapor-filled room, creating forms

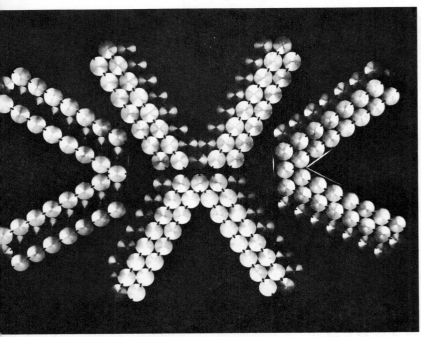

Tom Lloyd: *Veleuro, 1968,* multicolored programmed tail-lights; 78 inches wide. Wise Gallery, New York.

John Healey: *Box 3,* 1967, 38 inches wide. Sharp forms appear through back projection on a screen. Waddell Gallery.

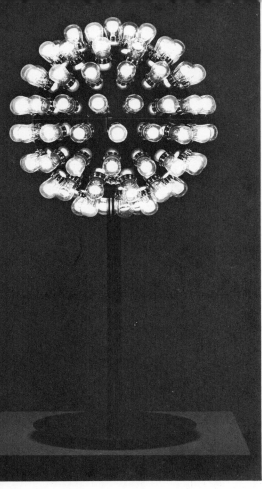

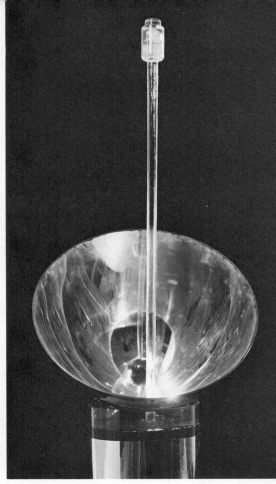

Otto Piene: *Electric Flower,* 1967, aluminum globe with 100 programmed bulbs, 16 inches diameter. Walker Art Center.

Stanley Landsman: *Albuquerque,* 1968, fluorescent tubes in mirror-lined box. Castelli Gallery.

Kosice: *Reflection and Linear Movement of Water,* 1967, plexiglas and water, 33½ inches high. Bonino Gallery, New York.

Billy Apple: *Solar 15,* 1966, neon wired to hang freely in space. Wheel is 30½ inches in diameter. Wise Gallery.

James Turrell's monochromatic "light-objects" are cast on blank walls by high-intensity projectors: *Afrum,* 1968.

Literal Light

that verged upon illusions of weight and solidity or planes.

Under the sub-heading Direct Light we have the fewest available examples. Dan Flavin's remarkable arrangements of fluorescent light fixtures are of the highest quality and set a standard by which to measure all other Light Art. Flavin's art, as pure as it is, still affords some interest in terms of the fixtures themselves. On the other hand, Les Levine's *White Sight,* shown recently at Fischbach, minimized even the fixtures. The piece consisted of the light cast in an empty room by two high-intensity monochromatic sodium vapor lights. The light itself was the piece. It had the peculiar characteristic of draining all color from the environment. All who entered the room looked as if they had just stepped out of a yellowed black-and-white photograph.

One other characteristic of electric lights is that they can be turned on and off. With few exceptions this characteristic has resulted in works more suitable to amusement parks or department store displays than for galleries or museums. The exceptions I wish to point out would be Takis's *Signals* and some neon works by Chryssa and Stephen Antonakos. The use of neon and of color are still other areas of Light Art open to continuing investigation.

It seems to me that Light Art, after several false starts, may be at a new beginning. We do not need more Light Art

Lila Katzen: *Moon Markers* environment, 1969, with NASA photos, black-light fixtures, mixed hard and soft fluorescent materials.

George Segal's plaster "tableau vivant" with neon sign: *Dry Cleaning Store,* 1964, life size. Janis Gallery, New York.

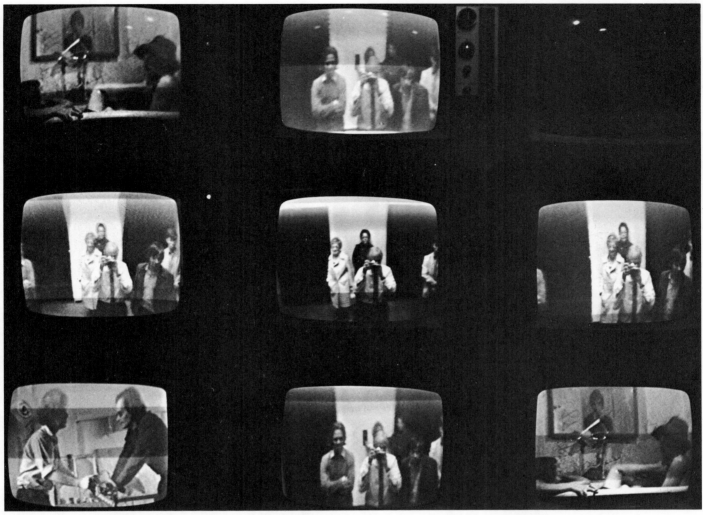

Frank Gillette and Ira Schneider: *Wipe Cycle,* 1969, 9 TV tubes which use a controlled sequence of videotapes of spectators, delayed playbacks of them, actual broadcasts and taped programs. Selected soundtracks are included. Wise Gallery.

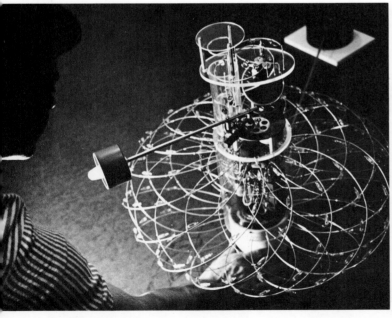

Delicate, hand-fashioned light work: Seawright's *Captive,* 1966, metal, plastic, electronic parts. Aldrich Museum, Ridgefield, Conn.

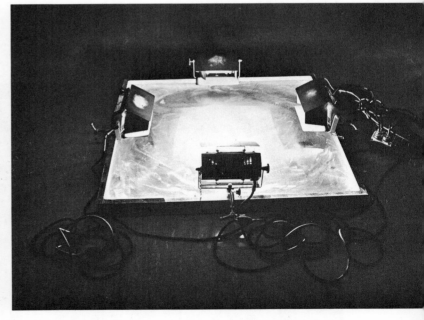

Bruce Nauman: *Lighted Centerpiece,* 1968, aluminum with four 1000-watt lamps, 36 inches square. Castelli Gallery.

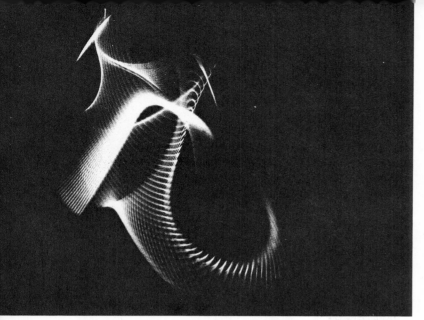

Three-dimensional ephemeral form: Nam June Paik 's *Holography-Horrography, Plus-Minus Silence.* Bonino Gallery, New York.

Literal Light

that is merely abstract cinema or discothèque decor and that falls short of the purity even of fireworks. We need further explorations of literal light. Light Art could be very important. At the moment it isn't. Its potentialities are obvious. The examples cited in this article offer some hope. The standards set by Minimal Art have certainly been a direct influence upon this new beginning. And now that younger artists are no longer thinking in terms of objects, the medium may yet come into its own. What we need now is more light, more consciousness, more intelligence in the creation of Light Art.

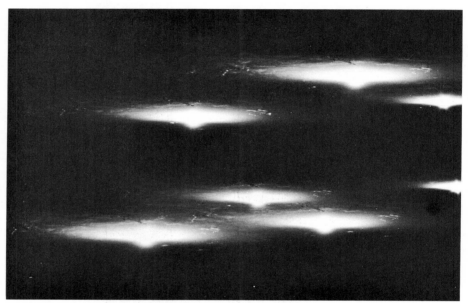

Mechanized Impressionism: the Pulsa group's underwater strobe lamps, at the Boston Gardens, 1968, palpitate in a pond.

Noise-making color: Howard Jones' *Time Columns—The Sound of Light,* 1968, stainless steel, multicolored bulbs, electronic sound. Wise Gallery.

Yaacov Agam's *Light Room,* 1968 contains one intensely bright bulb which is turned on by a sharp noise, such as a handcla Otherwise the room is pitch dar

By Aram Saroyan

Electric Poetry

By electric I mean instantaneous—
without any reading process at all;
and therefore continuous—
as the Present is —
without beginning, middle, or end.

Aram Saroyan is one of the best-known
of the young concrete poets. He is
the author of a book of poems, *Aram
Saroyan*, published by Random House.

night nigh

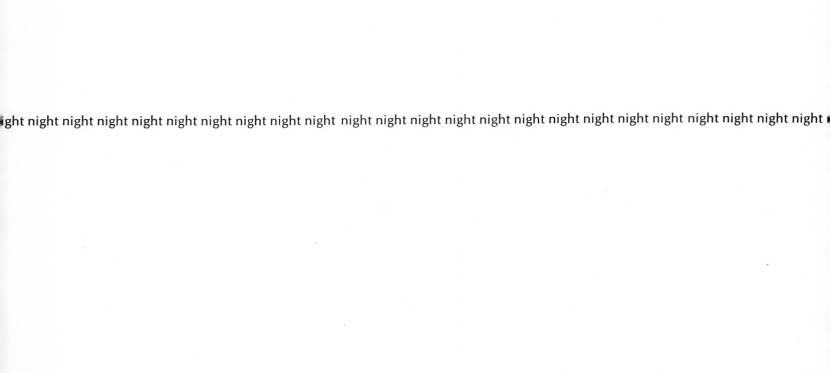

ight night night night night night night night night night night night night night night night night night night night night night

lighght

Index of Illustrations

Page numbers in italics indicates colorplates

Agam, Yaacov — *Light Room*, 141
Antonakos, Stephen — *Walk on Neon*, 134
Apple, Billy — *Solar 15*, 137
Bernini, Giovanni Lorenzo — *Cathedra Petri*, 102
Besoet, Jan — *Fireworks in an Outdoor Theater*, **128**
Bosch, Hieronymus — *Ascension of Souls to Paradise*, **125**
Creation of Eve, 108, detail, *111*
Seven Deadly Sins, detail, 124
Boudin, Eugène — *Dunquerque*, 68
Photograph of Boudin, 58
Burckhardt, Rudolph — *Flatiron Building*, 33
Button, John — *Blue Windows*, 32
Byzantine, altar — *Pala D'Oro*, 56
Byzantine, architecture — *Hagia Sophia*, 53
Byzantine, enamel — *Reliquary of the Cross*, **57**
Byzantine, gold — *Crown of Leo VI*, 55
Byzantine, icon — *Archangel Michael*, 46
Byzantine, manuscript — *Transfiguration*, 114
Byzantine, mosaic — *Adoration*, Sta. Maria Maggiore, **44**
Annunciation, Daphni, 54
Christ, Cefalù, 50
Christ, St. Peter's, 44
Constantine and Justinian, Hagìa **Sophia**, **52**
John Comnenus, Hagia Sophia, **52**
Leo VI, Hagia Sophia, 52
Pantocrator, Daphni, 51
Transfiguration, St. Catherine's **Monastery**, **48**
St. Porphyrios, Hagios Giorgios, *47*
Virgin, St. Sophia, Kiev, 49
Virgin and Child, Nicaea, 44
Campin, Robert — *Mérode Altarpiece*, detail, *110*
Nativity, 117
Caravaggio, Michelangelo da — *Calling of St. Matthew*, 96
Decollation of St. John the Baptist, **98, 99**
Christ at Emmaus, 100
Young Woman with a Violin, 107
Cézanne, Paul — *View of the Arc Valley*, 63
Chirico, Giorgio de — *The Disquieting Muses*, 74
Hector and Andromache, 72
Pink Tower, 75
Chryssa — *Untitled neon sculptures*, **132**
Constable, John — *The Hay Wain*, 66
Study of Sky and Trees, 66
Study of Tree Trunks, 70
Salisbury Cathedral from the Bishop's Garden, 6
View on the Stour, 69
Corot, Jean-Baptiste-Camille — *The Basilica of Constantine*, 65
The Mantes Bridge, 61
Courbet, Gustave — *A Forest Pool*, 67
Low Tide, 64
Dali, Salvador — *Sleep*, 78
Woman Sleeping in a Landscape, **78**
Daubigny, Charles François — *In the Woods*, 62
Daumier, Honoré — *Landscape Painters at Work*. 58
Delvaux, Paul — *Night Train*, 77
Nocturne, 77

Diaz, Narcisse — *Forest at Fontainebleau*, 61
Drummond, Sally Hazelet — *Beige Painting*, 31
Duchamp, Marcel — *The Bride Stripped Bare...*, **82**
Egyptian, obelisk — *Karnak*, 16
Egyptian, papyrus — *Princess Her-uben*, 18
Egyptian, pyramid — *Cheops*, 17
Cheops and Khefre, 8
Snefru, 17
Egyptian, relief — *Baboons worshipping the sun*, **12**
Osiris on bier, 12
Royal bust, 10
Tutankhamun's throne, 19
Egyptian, sculpture — *Khefre*, 12
Zoser, 12
Egyptian, temple — *Abu Simbel*, 15
Edfu, 13
Luxor, 14
Medinet Habu, 14
Ernst, Max — *Bird in the Heart of the Forest*, **79**
Europe after the Rain, 79
The Great Forest, 79
Estes, Richard — *Brownstone Reflections*, 32
Eyck, Jan van — *Berlin Madonna*, 108; detail, **112**
Flavin, Dan — *Pink and Gold*, 133
Fragonard, Jean Honoré — *The Avenue*, 60
French, manuscript — *Pan*, 122
Friedrich, Caspar David — *Meadows near Greifswald*, 64
Gaudi, Antonio — *Crucifix for Casa Battlo*, 87
Massacre of the Innocents, detail, **94, 95**
Mirror study for angel, 90
Mirror study for crèche, 90
Mirror study, female model, 89
Mirror study, model for Christ, 88
Photograph of the artist, 84
Photograph studies of skeletons, **86**
Portal of Charity, detail, 92, 93
Sagrada Familia, Barcelona, 84
Study for crucifix, 87
Geertgen tot Sint Jans — *Nativity*, 118
Gillette, Frank and Ira Schneider — *Wipe Cycle*, 139
Goes, Hugo van der — *Portinari Altarpiece*, details, 108, **121**
Gorky, Arshile — *Betrothal, I*, 83
The Plow and the Song, 27
Gothic, manuscript — *Ingeborg Psalter*, 42
Moralized Bible, detail, 36
Gothic, stained glass — *Cathedral of Leon*, Spain, *43*
Cathedral of Sées, 40
Chartres, 39
Ste.-Chapelle, Paris, 41
St.-Denis, 34, 42
Ste.-Foy de Conques, 41
St.-Gratien, Tours, 37, 38
St.-Pierre, Poitiers, 36
Grünewald, Matthias — *Resurrected Christ*, 7; detail, cover
Guston, Philip — *Painting*, 25
Hart, Gordon — *Untitled*, 28

Healey, John — Box 3, 136
Hofmann, Hans — Memoria in Aeternum, 25
Honthorst, Gerrit van — The Matchmaker, 96
Honthorst (attributed) — Supper at Emmaus, 100
Hopper, Edward — Seven A.M., 20
Humphrey, Ralph — Untitled, 31
Jones, Howard — Time Columns, 140
Katzen, Lila — Moon Markers, 138
Kelly, Ellsworth — Blue Green Red 1, 29
Klapheck, Konrad — War, 83
Klausenburg, Thomas von — The Resurrection, 123
Kline, Franz — New York, 20
Night Square, 20
Kooning, Willem de — Rosy-Fingered Dawn at Louse Point, 22
Kosice, Gyula — Reflection and Movement of Water, 137
Landsman, Stanley — Albuquerque, 137
La Tour, Georges de — St. Peter Denying Christ, 96
Levine, Les — Standard Equipment, 135
Lichtenstein, Roy — Modern Painting Diptych, 30
Lloyd, Tom — Veleuro, 136
Lorrain, Claude (Gellée) — The Judgment of Paris, 103
Louis, Morris — Floral, 26
Magritte, René — Domain of Lights, 4
Domain of Lights, 2, 72
Memory of a Voyage, 76
Personal Values, 76
Manet, Edouard — Monet Painting in His Studio-Boat, 71
Marquet, Albert — Pont St. Michel, 69
Martin, Agnes — The City, 31
Masson, André — Meditation on an Oak Leaf, 83
Master of Aachener Schranktüren — The Miracle of St. Bruno, detail, 113
Master of St. Giles — The Mass of St. Giles, 116
Master of St. Ursula — Dream of the Saint, 119
Matta — The Bachelors Twenty Years After, 82
Vertigo of Eros, 83
Miro, Joan — Portrait of Mrs. Mills in 1750, 81
Still-life with Old Shoe, 81
Moholy-Nagy, Laszlo — Light-Space Modulator, 130
Monet, Claude — The Four Poplars, 63
Rouen Cathedral, West Façade, 69
Nauman, Bruce — Lighted Centerpiece, 139
Newman, Barnett — Vir Heroicus Sublimis, 24
Noland, Kenneth — Stria, 26
Paik, Nam June — Holography-Horrography . . . , 140
Piene, Otto — Electric Flower, 137
Pissarro, Camille — The Hermitage Road, Pontoise, 62
Pollock, Jackson — Lucifer, 28
Poons, Larry — Richmond Ruckus, 30
Poussin, Nicholas — Landscape with St. Matthew, 61
Pulsa — Underwater strobes, 140
Ray, Man — The Primacy of Matter over Mind, 78
Reinhardt, Ad — Untitled, 24
Rembrandt van Rijn — The Circumcision of Christ, 104
Margaretha de Geer, Wife of Jacob Trip, 101
Rosa, Salvator — Mercury and the Dishonest Woodsman, 104
Night Scene with Figures, 105

Rothko, Mark — No. 8, 1952, 23
Rubens, Peter Paul — Abraham and Melchizedek, 103
Ryman, Robert — Standard, 31
Sargent, John Singer — Monet Painting in his Studio-Boat, 71
Seawright, James — Captive, 139
Segal, George — Dry Cleaning Store, 138
Signorelli, Luca — Education of Pan, 126
Sisley, Alfred — Landscape: Snow Effect, 68
Stella, Frank — Ophir, 28
Swain, Robert — Untitled, No. 2, 29
Tanguy, Yves — Imaginary Numbers, 80
Mama, Papa is Wounded!, 72
Turrell, James — Afrum, 137
Tuttle, Richard — Canvas, 27
Valenciennes, Pierre-Henry de — At the Villa Farnese, 65
Vermeer, Jan — Woman in Blue Reading a Letter, 106
Watteau, Jean Antoine — The Minuet in a Pavilion, 60
Wilfred, Thomas — Aspiration, Op. 145, 131

Photograph Credits

Cover: transparency Eric Schaal, courtesy Life magazine. 12: Hirmer (Phaidon). 13: Office du Livre, Fribourg (Grosset & Dunlap). 14: Kim Levin; Office du Livre. 15: Dr. Georg Gertser, Zurich. 16, 17: Office du Livre; Brooklyn Museum Archives. 34, 41: Archives Photographiques, Paris. 36: British Museum; Reynal & Co; William Morrow & Co. 37, 38: Gudiol, Barcelona. 39: Bildarchiv Foto Marburg. 39: Roger-Viollet, Paris. 40: Arthaud, Paris. 43, 50: Editions d'Art Albert Skira, Geneva. 44: Phototeca Unione, Rome. 46, 47: Hirmer Fotoarchiv, Munich. 48: Michigan-Princeton-Alexandria Expedition to Mt. Sinai. 49: Novosti Press Agency, New York. 51, 53: Josephine Powell, Rome. 52: Dumbarton Oaks Research Library, Washington, D.C. 54, 56: Osvaldo Böhm, Venice. 57: Bildarchiv Foto-Marburg. 86, 90: Juan Matamala Archives. 87: Ferran Archives; Friends of Gaudi. 88: Gazette des Arts. 89, 90: A. Opisso Archives. 91: Ferran Archives. 102: Leonard von Matt, Buochs, Switzerland. 113, 118: Rhenische Bildarchiv, Köln. 114: Hirmer Fotoarchiv, Munich. 115: Conzett & Huber, Zurich. 126: Hanfstaengl, Munich. 137: Newsweek— Dee Gorton. 138: Robert A. Propper. 141: Kineticism Press, New York.

New AND Exciting
BOOKS FROM ABRAMS

REMBRANDT: His Life, His Work, His Time *by Bob Haak.* 612 illustrations, 109 hand-tipped plates in full color, maps and chart, 348 pages, 10⅝ x 13⅝" $35.00

PICASSO: His Recent Drawings/1966-1968 *by Charles Feld. With a preface by René Char.* 405 illustrations, 27 in full color and 32 in duotone, 248 pages, 9½ x 11⅜". $25.00

SELF-PORTRAIT: U.S.A. *by David Douglas Duncan.* Here is the drama, violence, pageantry, and excitement of America making its political choice during our two national conventions—brought into startling focus by the penetrating words and pictures of David Douglas Duncan. 325 black-and-white photographs, 240 pages, 11 x 14". $18.50

SEURAT *by Pierre Courthion.* 125 illustrations, 48 hand-tipped in full color, 160 pages, 9¾ x 13". $15.00

JUAN GRIS *by Daniel-Henry Kahnweiler.* 184 illustrations, 24 in full color, 348 pages, 9⅝ x 11¾". $25.00

THE COMPLETE WORKS OF MARCEL DUCHAMP *by Arturo Schwarz.* 760 illustrations, 75 hand-tipped plates in full color, 650 pages, 10¼ x 12¼". $50.00

MARCEL DUCHAMP: Notes and Projects for the Large Glass *by Arturo Schwarz.* 206 pages of facsimile notes with translations, 10 x 16½". $35.00

RUBENS' LIFE OF MARIE DE' MEDICI *by Jacques Thuillier and Jacques Foucart.* 160 hand-tipped illustrations, 108 in full color, 250 pages, 12¾ x 15⅞". $150.00

DADA AND SURREALIST ART *by William S. Rubin.* 851 illustrations, 60 in full color, 525 pages, 9⅝ x 11¾". $35.00

ROBERT RAUSCHENBERG *by Andrew Forge.* 153 illustrations, 47 in full color, 226 pages, 11⅜ x 10⅝". $25.00

HISTORY OF ITALIAN RENAISSANCE ART *by Frederick Hartt.* 811 illustrations, 80 in full color, 592 pages, 8¾ x 11½". $25.00

MODIGLIANI DRAWINGS AND SKETCHES *by Franco Russoli.* 100 illustrations, 4 in full color, 132 pages, 10⅝ x 12⅝". $20.00

ART OF ANCIENT EGYPT *by Kazimierz Michalowski.* 904 illustrations, 145 in full color, 135 plans, elevations, sites, and diagrams, 15 maps and charts, 600 pages. 9½ x 12⅛". $40.00

PRE-COLUMBIAN ART OF MEXICO AND CENTRAL AMERICA *by Hasso von Winning.* 595 illustrations, 175 hand-tipped in full color, 388 pages, 10 x 13". $35.00

MICHELANGELO: The Complete Sculpture *by Frederick Hartt.* 332 illustrations, 18 hand-tipped plates in full color, 312 pages. 9½ x 12⅝". $20.00

BONNARD *by André Fermigier.* 128 illustrations, 49 hand-tipped in full color, 160 pages, 9¾ x 13". $17.50

EVOLUTION OF MODERN SCULPTURE: Tradition and Innovation *by A. M. Hammacher.* 404 illustrations, 27 in full color, 384 pages, 9⅞ x 12⅝". $25.00

RICHARD LINDNER *by Dore Ashton.* 187 illustrations, 52 hand-tipped plates in full color, 218 pages, 11⅜ x 10⅝". $25.00

BEN NICHOLSON: Drawings, Paintings, and Reliefs. *Introduction by John Russell.* 298 illustrations, 78 hand-tipped plates in full color, 324 pages, 11⅜ x 13". $35.00

PREHISTORIC AND PRIMITIVE ART *by Luis Pericot-Garcia, John Galloway, and Andreas Lommel.* 489 illustrations, 51 in full color, 340 pages, 9 x 12½". $25.00

ADVENTURE IN ART: An International Group of Art Collections in Industrial Environments. *Foreword by Lord Robbins,* C.B., *Introduction by Milton S. Fox.* 149 illustrations in full color, 232 pages, 11¾ x 11¾". $40.00

CLASSICS OF THE WORLD'S GREAT ART

Each title contains 200 black-and-white illustrations, 64 pages in full color, 116 pages, 9 x 12½". $5.95 each. Volumes present THE COMPLETE PAINTINGS OF:

BOSCH Introduction by Gregory Martin
BRUEGEL Introduction by Robert Hughes
CARAVAGGIO Introduction by Michael Kitson
GIOTTO Introduction by Andrew Martindale
LEONARDO DA VINCI Introduction by L. D. Ettlinger
MANET Introduction by Phoebe Pool
MICHELANGELO Introduction by L. D. Ettlinger
RAPHAEL Introduction by Richard Cooke
THE VAN EYCKS Introduction by Robert Hughes
VERMEER Introduction by John Jacob

PANORAMA OF WORLD ART SERIES
Each title 264 pages, 7½ x 8¾" $7.95 each

New titles:

PREHISTORIC EUROPEAN ART *by Walter Torbrügge.* 292 illustrations, 175 in full color.

ART OF CRETE, MYCENAE, AND GREECE *by German Hafner.* 267 illustrations, 140 in full color.

ART OF THE ANCIENT NEAR AND MIDDLE EAST *by C. J. Du Ry.* 250 illustrations, 150 in full color.

BAROQUE AND ROCOCO ART *by Liselotte Andersen.* 261 illustrations, 161 in full color.

Write for free copy of new large (9x12") color catalogue. More than 300 superlative books profusely illustrated and described.

HARRY N. ABRAMS, INC.
TIMES MIRROR
The world's largest publisher of books on the fine arts

110 E. 59th St., New York, N.Y. 10022

Morris Broderson

Still Life with Japanese Bowl   1969

30 x 40"   Watercolor

Collection Mr. and Mrs. Deane Johnson   Bel Air

ANKRUM GALLERY   LOS ANGELES   THE DOWNTOWN GALLERY   NEW YORK

Marlborough-Gerson Gallery Inc
41 East 57th Street   New York

Mordecai Ardon
Allan D'Arcangelo
Naum Gabo
Juan Genovés
Adolph Gottlieb
Philip Guston
R B Kitaj
Lee Krasner
Jacques Lipchitz
Seymour Lipton
Conrad Marca-Relli
Gerhard Marcks
Robert Motherwell
Beverly Pepper
Larry Rivers
James Rosati
Mark Rothko
Julius Schmidt
Jesus Raphael Soto
Michael Steiner
Clyfford Still
James Wines
Fritz Wotruba
The Estate of William Baziotes
The Estate of Lyonel Feininger
The Estate of Franz Kline
The Estate of John Marin
The Estate of Jackson Pollock
The Estate of Ad Reinhardt
The Estate of David Smith

Marlborough Fine Art (London) Ltd
39 Old Bond Street   London W1

Craigie Aitchison
Michael Andrews
Kenneth Armitage
Frank Auerbach
Francis Bacon
Lynn Chadwick
Lucian Freud
Günter Haese
Barbara Hepworth
Oskar Kokoschka
Leon Kossoff
Colin Lanceley
Richard Lin
Lucebert
Meier-Denninghoff
Henry Moore
Sidney Nolan
Victor Pasmore
Roland Piché
John Piper
Paul Rebeyrolle
Ceri Richards
Edward Seago
Colin Self
Jack Smith
Graham Sutherland
Joe Tilson
Keith Vaughan
Brett Whiteley
The Estate of Willi Baumeister
The Estate of David Bomberg
The Estate of Kurt Schwitters

Marlborough Galleria d'Arte
via Gregoriana 5   Rome

Piero Dorazio
Achille Perilli
Arnaldo Pomodoro
Toti Scialoia
The Estate of Spazzapan
The Estate of Fontana

Marlborough
NEW YORK · LONDON · ROME

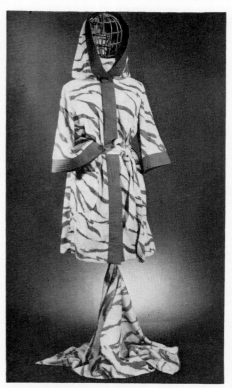

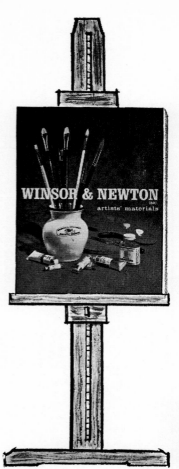

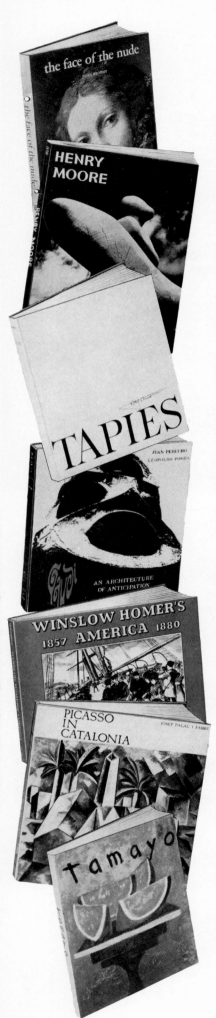

The Finest in Recent Art Books

THE FACE OF THE NUDE. By John Brophy. Large reproductions of facial detail appearing opposite 102 rich color plates of the complete works by Botticelli, Leonardo et al. A unique comparative study. *9x11½"*   **9.95**

HENRY MOORE. By Ionel Jianou. A telling biography and incisive analysis of the world's most popular sculptor. With an extensive catalogue raisonné of Moore's finest work. *8½x11"   121 full-page plates.*   **15.00**

TAPIES. By Blai Bonet. Spain's contemporary master of abstract painting and one of the most potently creative artists of our time. *10½x12"   100 plates, 25 in color.*   **37.50**

GAUDI. By Juan Perucho. A brilliant, intuitive technique that architecture is only now appreciating. With photos and structural plans of Gaudi's most daring works. *10⅞x10⅞"   133 plates, 43 in color.*   **25.00**

WINSLOW HOMER'S AMERICA. By Lloyd Goodrich. A whole era in American life portrayed in 156 masterful wood engravings that rank with the best of Homer's paintings. *9½x12½"*   **15.00**

PICASSO IN CATALONIA. By Josep Palau i Fabre. Reveals for the first time the obscure, intimate aspects of Picasso's Spanish heritage. *10½x10½"   217 plates, 72 in color.*   **25.00**

TAMAYO. Intro. by Juan Garcia Ponce. Mexico's greatest abstract modernist in 64 reproductions, 35 in lavish color. *10x14" portfolio volume.*   **30.00**

BERNARD BUFFET. *Lithographs 1952-1966.* Compiled by Fernand Mourlot. 66 beautiful works reproduced in the same number of colors as the rare originals, plus 11 lithographs drawn especially for this volume. *9½x12½"*   **37.50**

DICTIONARY OF MODERN PAINTING. Ed. Carlton Lake and Robert Maillard. Full information on every major painter and style since Impressionism. *470 reproductions, 375 in full color.*   **8.95**

JOAN MIRO AND CATALONIA. By Juan Perucho. The vital relationship between one of this century's greats and his native land. *Hundreds of plates, 86 in brilliant color. 10-7/16x10⅞"*   **25.00**

SIQUEIROS. Intro. by Enrique Gual. Portfolio-sized volume containing 32 sumptuous color reproductions of works by Mexico's foremost living artist. *11x15"*   **25.00**

1900 IN BARCELONA *(Art Nouveau).* By A. Cirici Pellicer. The birthplace of Modernismo and one of the richest centers of Art Nouveau in the world. *7⅞ x 7⅞"   88 plates, 21 in beautiful color.*   **12.50**

PICASSO LINOCUTS. By Donald H. Karshan. One of the most important graphic arts innovations of our time—a virtually complete collection of Picasso's work in the one block, multi-color linoleum print. *10x8½"   100 plates, 22 in color.*   **7.95**

ALPHONSE MUCHA. By Jiri Mucha. The foremost propagist of Art Nouveau. Reproduces over 300 of Mucha's most decorative posters, designs etc. *9x11"   32 color plates.*   **15.00**

Tudor Publishing Company
572 Fifth Avenue, New York 10036

155

The Magnificent Marketplace

Where Rembrandt's "Aristotle" shattered the previous auction price record, making headlines around the world. Where Richard Burton won the famed Krupp diamond ring for Mrs. Burton. Where, only weeks after its discovery, one of eight known original copies of the U.S. Constitution made history again by changing hands. This is Parke-Bernet, the nation's foremost art auction gallery. Truly a magnificent marketplace.

This pre-eminence did not just occur. It was achieved by conscientious development of all that goes to make *the* leading auction gallery in the U.S. Unsurpassed facilities —for exhibiting, for auctioning. Desirable, comprehensive services—*appraisals* for estate tax, insurance and other purposes; authoritative *catalogues* available individually or to subscribers by category; Auction Magazine with scholarly and entertaining articles as well as copious listings of current auction prices. And, *PB-84*, a new branch gallery in Manhattan offering a vast assortment of articles in more informal surroundings.

One result of this unique combination of services is a large and dedicated clientele the world over. To help serve it better, Parke-Bernet maintains offices in Houston, Beverly Hills, Denver, Toronto, Paris, Munich, Florence, Beirut, Melbourne and Johannesburg. Affiliation with Sotheby & Company, London, provides a choice of sale locations—New York or London.

Parke-Bernet—the magnificent marketplace—for buying, as well as selling, antiquities, rare books, manuscripts and autographs, paintings, drawings and sculpture of all schools, prints from Old Masters to Moderns, furniture, rugs and decorations, porcelains, glass, paperweights, works of art, objects de vertu, watches, Oriental art, silver and silver plate, jewelry, coins and antique cars.

For details on subscribing to catalogues—or on selling property at auction, write Parke-Bernet.

Parke-Bernet
GALLERIES • INC

980 Madison Avenue, New York 10021 • Peter Wilson, Chairman/Peregrine Pollen, President • Affiliated with Sotheby & Co., London

157

LARRY ZOX 1970

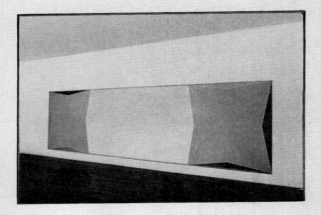

Kornblee 58 e 79 NYC

Reliquary Figure
Fang, Gabon
18¼" high

Primitive and Modern Arts

Merton D. Simpson

1063 Madison Avenue at 80th
New York City 10028
212 YUkon 8-6290

RICHARD
DIEBENKORN
OCEAN PARK SERIES

POINDEXTER
24 EAST 84th STREET
NEW YORK, N. Y. 10028

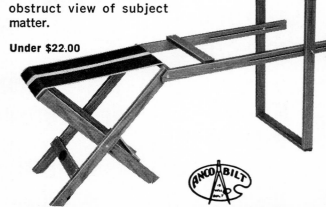

CLEVELAND INSTITUTE OF ART

PROFESSIONAL TRAINING

Painting   Sculpture
Printmaking
Industrial Design
Graphic Design
Photography
Ceramics
Weaving   Textiles
Silversmithing
Enameling
Teacher Training

DEGREES-SCHOLARSHIPS
CATALOG ON REQUEST
Write: Director of Admissions,
11141 East Boulevard,
Cleveland, Ohio 44106

BOSTON...
is an Art Center

- ■ faculty of professional artists
- ■ bachelor's and master's degrees
- ■ painting ■ sculpture
- ■ art education
- ■ advertising design
- ■ interior design
- ■ summer programs at Tanglewood

BOSTON UNIVERSITY

School of Fine and Applied Arts
855 Commonwealth Avenue
Boston, Mass. 02215

AN INDEPENDENT PROFESSIONAL ART SCHOOL IN HIGHER EDUCATION

Fine Arts
Advertising Arts
Photography
Film
Humanities

SCHOOL OF VISUAL ARTS

209 EAST 23RD STREET, NEW YORK, N.Y. 10010

THE ART STUDENTS LEAGUE OF NEW YORK

215 W. 57th St., N.Y. 10019
CIrcle 7-4510
Stewart Klonis, Director

Now in its 95th year, the League continues to offer many courses in **painting, drawing, sculpture** (traditional as well as all phases of direct metal sculpture), **illustration, graphics, textile design, commercial art, and mural painting.** Registration by the month: different points of view represented on staff of **51 famous artist-instructors**; five-day, two-day and single day classes, weekly, in A.M., P.M. and Eve. sessions; also Saturday classes; and Summer Schools in New York City and in Woodstock.

Illustrated catalogue on request.

Instructors

Barbara Adrian	Dagmar Freuchen	Kay Lewis
Charles Alston	Henry Gasser	Andrew Lukach
Lennart Anderson	Marshall Glasier	Vincent Malta
Rudolf Baranik	Peter Golfinopoulos	Frank Mason
Will Barnet	John Groth	Earl Mayan
Robert Brackman	Robert B. Hale	Edward Melcarth
Raymond Breinin	Agnes Hart	Seong Moy
Mario Cooper	Felrath Hines	S. Edmund Oppenheim
Jose de Creeft	Al Hollingsworth	Anthony Palumbo
Ben Cunningham	John Hovannes	Robert Philipp
Gregory D'Alessio	Morris Kantor	Michael Ponce de Leon
Roberto De Lamonica	Ethel Katz	Larry Poons
Sidney E. Dickinson	Nathaniel Kaz	Robert Emil Schulz
William F. Draper	Steven Kidd	Patricia Sherwood
Jack Faragasso	William King	Theodoros Stamos
Thomas Fogarty	Edward Laning	Willa Trafton
Arthur J. Foster	Julian Levi	Vaclav Vytlacil

Sound good

Don't take the fifth; take the lead with a quote from Newsweek, the newsweekly that other communications media quote on the largest scale. Score with a key fact from our news columns. Or strike a responsive chord with a measured opinion from one of our columnists.

Then be prepared to take a bow.

quote
Newsweek / the newsweekly that separates fact from opinion

TO THE KING'S TASTE

The frame illustrated is our model #15-418-S. In carved and gilded wood, it is an exact copy of a fine original of the Louis XV period.

This and scores of other examples of A.P.F. craftsmanship are now available and may be seen in

BOSTON
Roger Lussier
115 Newbury Street

CHICAGO
The Frame Shop, Inc.
230 East Ohio Street

MIAMI
Dimensions
3195 Commodore Plaza
Coconut Grove

A.P.F., Inc.,

SHOWROOMS:
231 East 60 Street
&
1001 Madison Avenue

FACTORY & OFFICE:
315 East 91 Street
New York City

Master Framemakers & Conservators

AQUATEC, THE ARTISTS ACRYLIC

Water based. Deep. Brilliant. Permanent. Aquatec is the world's finest acrylic artist color. Made of 100% acrylic polymer emulsion that makes it possible for artists to explore new and expressive techniques from delicate, transparent washes, to heaviest impasto. **Special Introductory Offer:** a working palette of 11 studio-size colors, plus Aquatec Jel and a King-size tube of Titanium White, only $7.75.* Check or money-order...no COD's. For color chart and full information write Bocour Artist Colors, Inc. 552 West 52 Street, New York 10019. (In Canada, Heinz-Jordan Ltd., 42 Gladstone Rd., Toronto 3.) Aquatec is available at leading art supply stores everywhere.   *NYC residents add 6% Sales Tax.

Do you know about THE AMERICAN FEDERATION OF ARTS?

10 THINGS AFA DOES:

1 subsidizes and circulates *exhibitions* of painting, sculpture and architecture for small museums, colleges and art centers. Last year it had more than 468 showings of 90 different exhibitions throughout the United States **2** publishes *books* and *catalogs* of lasting importance, not only catalogs of exhibitions **3** produces a *curriculum of visual education* for elementary and secondary schools and organizes and circulates a program of *films on art* **4** promotes international goodwill through the *exchange of exhibitions* with Europe and the Far East **5** plans *educational tours* to little known culture areas throughout the world **6** arranges through an *anonymous donor program* for the purchase of works of art for museums with limited funds **7** conducts an *art critics work-shop* **8** invites contributions from industry for the encouragement of painting, sculpture and the decorative arts **9** is piloting a project for rehabilitating the handwork industries of impoverished Appalachia **10** actively supports legislation which is beneficial to the art world.

10 REASONS FOR JOINING AFA

$18 ANNUAL MEMBERSHIP ENTITLES YOU TO:

1 Complimentary annual subscription to *The Art Gallery*
2 25 percent discount on most art books
3 Opportunity to participate in the renowned domestic and foreign art tours specifically tailored for AFA members
4 Special discounts on 26 magazines related to the arts
5 20 percent discount on membership in International Graphic Arts Society
6 Special discounts on AFA Reference Books: *The American Art Directory* and *Who's Who in American Art*
7 Special rates for subscriptions to *Art News, Arts* and *Art International*
8 Invitation to Openings of AFA Exhibitions and announcements of special art events
9 Invitations to AFA Meetings and Symposia
10 The satisfaction of supporting the most vital and far-reaching art organization in the United States today

Detach coupon and mail now

- -

MEMBERS WHO CONTRIBUTE $35 or more in Annual Dues receive in addition to all other benefits: Free annual subscriptions to *two* of three leading magazines, *Art in America, Art News,* and *Art International, catalogs of distinctive AFA exhibitions* distributed periodically, and a ticket admitting *TWO* to *special* events of outstanding interest.

MEMBERS WHO CONTRIBUTE $65 or more in Annual Dues, in addition to all other benefits as listed above, receive a complimentary copy of *Art News Annual,* all volumes issued in the AFA *Special Publication Series* and on request may be enrolled as members of the *International Graphic Arts Society.*

☐ $ 18 Active
☐ $ 35 Contributing
☐ $ 65 Supporting
☐ $100 Sustaining
☐ $250 Sponsor
☐ $500 Patron

($35 and over please CHECK TWO magazines)
☐ Art News
☐ Art in America
☐ Art International

NAME . . . .

ADDRESS . . . .

CITY . . . . STATE . . . . ZIP . . . .

ana

THE AMERICAN FEDERATION OF ARTS, 41 E. 65th St., New York, N. Y. 10021

The American Federation of Arts was founded in 1909. Incorporated in 1916 as a non-profit educational organization.
SUPPORT THIS NATIONAL ART ORGANIZATION THROUGH MEMBERSHIP